ANCIENT PATHS *for* MODERN WOMEN

Walking in the Church & in the World

JUDY GERRY

LifeSong
PUBLISHERS

ANCIENT PATHS
MINISTRIES

ISBN 0-9718306-5-7

Copyright 2004 by LifeSong Publishers
All rights reserved

Published by LifeSong Publishers
P.O. Box 183, Somis, CA 93066-0183
805-655-5644
www.lifesongpublishers.com

Unless otherwise noted, all Bible quotations used in this study are taken from the New American Standard Bible.

Scripture taken from the NEW AMERICAN STANDARD BIBLE. Copyright 1960, 1962, 1963, 1968, 1971, 1972, 1973, 1975, 1977, 1995 by the Lockman Foundation. Used by permission.

Holy Bible: New International Version. Copyright 1978 by the New York International Bible Society.

Webster's New World College Dictionary, Third Edition, Simon & Schuster, Inc., 1997.

Illustrations by Wendy Kappen
Cover design by Jeff Sharpton and Jon Walusiak at Design Point
Cover photo by Comstock.com
Printed in the United States of America

First Edition
Library of Congress Control Number: 2003111864
p.134 cm. 25.4

TABLE OF CONTENTS

Endorsements

"Being born female in today's western world frequently offers a false sense of confidence. Armed with education and unprecedented privilege, women are writing their own scripts about family and personal fulfillment, but later encounter confusion and bleak emptiness. Having been taught to disregard the wisdom of their Creator, they bypass the solutions they seek.

Judy Gerry has dug deeply into the sacred records of the Bible to surface divine guidance for women in every generation. Here is a timely, reassuring and professionally crafted study resource which belongs in every church library and on the study agenda for thinking women."

Howard G. Hendricks
Distinguished Professor and Chairman, Center for Christian Leadership
Dallas Theological Seminary

"Judy Gerry has a long-time track record of walking with the Lord as a woman and as a wife and mother. For many years, she has had an effective ministry of training women in the Word and ways of God. Now her years of study and experience are combined in this practical, interactive course designed to help women understand God's purpose and plan for their lives.

Judy does not claim to offer new or original ideas. Rather, she leads women to discover and apply the tried, true, and enduring way laid out for us in the Scripture– the pathway that leads to blessing and joy.

In a day when so many Christian women are floundering and confused, the wisdom found in this program is timely and desperately needed. I pray this course will be widely received and will be used to bring about a true revolution in the hearts and homes of women who profess to know Christ."

Nancy Leigh DeMoss
Author; Host of Revive Our Hearts Radio

"I love "*Ancient Paths for Modern Women*" because it takes women to the Bible! His Word changes lives! I have observed tearful testimonies of women coming to Christ, marriages healed, children raised according to God's plan, repentance revived, and church problems solved. Today's women are so thirsty to hear God's Word. After teaching *Ancient Paths* this summer to forty women, I again stand in awe as I have watched God work through this study. "

Linda Campbell
Bible Study Leader
Actively Serving in Women's Ministries in Ventura County

Preface

Millennia ago God set out ancient paths for us to walk, which would lead us to abundant life, and into perfect fellowship with Himself. The Lord promised us that when we see and walk in that "good way" that we will find rest for our souls.

"Thus says the LORD,
'Stand by the ways and see and ask for the ancient paths,
where the good way is, and walk in it;
and you shall find rest for your souls.'"
Jeremiah 6:16

Contemporary women have veered sharply from the "good way" that God has intended for us to live. While longing for elusive rest for their souls, women have rejected God's pathways as being too simplistic and archaic. Sensing that something is wrong, we are unable to grasp how grossly off track we are.

Many Christian women have "stumbled from the ancient paths" by believing various ideas and secular concepts which are not biblical (Jeremiah 18:15). Lives are being diminished by disobedience, and it truly breaks our Father's heart.

Many women are walking in darkness. In order to dispel the darkness we need to turn on the light. God has told us that His Word will light our path (Psalm 119:105). The goal of this study is to discern God's will for women as we learn what Scripture reveals about women of the Word.

As a young mother in the 1970's, I encountered scores of good Bible studies dealing with being a woman of God. Today there are only a few to be found, yet there is an increasingly dire need for teaching biblical mandates for women.

Through the strong and helpful encouragement of my husband, Dave, and the enthusiastic support of our five children, the Lord led me in preparing this material. Special thanks to the many women who have continually encouraged me, and to Dave who has spent countless hours formatting these materials.

While preparing this study I learned much, and the Lord has used His Word to exhort and challenge me to personal spiritual growth. My prayer is that as you dig into the Word, you will become conformed to the image of Christ.

"For I am confident of this very thing, that He who began a good work in you will perfect it until the day of Christ Jesus. For it is only right for me to feel this way about you all, because I have you in my heart..."
Philippians 1:6, 7a

Judy

How to Use This Study

During this study we will focus on God's specific directives for women. Taking biblical commands and precepts one by one, our goal will be to determine what God is telling us to do, and to explore how they are practical for the "nitty-gritty" of daily living.

How do women of the Word go about living in this world today? *Ancient Paths for Modern Women* is a four-part discipleship program designed to be most effective when studied in sequence.

- **Ancient Paths I- Walking With the Lord** (seven weeks), addresses how to develop an intimate, personal walk with the Lord.

- **Ancient Paths II- Walking as Wives** (seven weeks), leads us to learn and apply what God says about women walking as wives in the marriage relationship.

- **Ancient Paths III- Walking as Mothers and Homemakers** (seven weeks), examines the Lord's desire for women as they disciple their children and build God-honoring homes.

- **Ancient Paths IV- Walking in the Church and in the World** (eight weeks), grapples with issues related to God's will for women in the church, a woman's walk in the secular world, and how to keep walking faithfully.

It is preferable to have each chapter's work completed prior to the Bible study time. Many chapters have questions marked "***Optional.***" If you choose to answer those questions you will need additional Bible study resource books. A description of these is located at the back of this study.

You will notice that each page has a "Prayer Points" area provided in the margin. This is designed for use in jotting down ideas, items for discussion, questions, group prayer requests, or personal prayer needs that the Holy Spirit may bring to mind during the study.

The last page of each chapter is best handled in a small group format. It is recommended that you complete and record your "Summary," "Discussion" and "Application" responses prior to the lesson so that you can share your answers and ideas.

It is suggested that you use the chapter heading as a type of filing system. It may be a notebook with pockets or a portable file. As time goes by, insert current events, magazine articles, and even cartoons into the appropriate chapter topic. Be alert for other applicable Scripture to insert in various chapters. The long-term goal is that you will be able to teach and encourage other women as you mature in the Lord using the enclosed materials.

⌘   ⌘   ⌘

Ancient Paths Bible Study Series is especially effective when used by "older women" as they mentor "younger women." The long-term goal of this study is that you will be able to teach and encourage other women as you both mature in the Lord.

"Come, Walk the Ancient Paths"

Come and walk the ancient paths	(Jeremiah 6:16)
That lead into the Savior's heart.	(Revelation 19:7)
His Word reveals the wisdom past	(Proverbs 4:11)
Of just one Way to life and rest,	(John 14:6)
So choose this route and start.	(Deuteronomy 30:19)
Come, walk the road that leads to joy,	(Psalm 16:11)
And though the trail may steepen,	(James 1:2)
The obstacles of Satan's ploys	(Ephesians 6:10-13)
Thrust us on Jesus to employ	(II Corinthians 12:9, 10)
His grace, which daily deepens.	(Hebrews 4:16)
Come, run by grace, the ancient race,	(Hebrews 12:1)
Intent to win the prize.	(I Corinthians 9:24)
The goal in view is Jesus' face;	(Hebrews 12:1)
Press on, reach out, pick up the pace	(Philippians 3:13, 14)
Toward heaven set your eyes.	(Hebrews 12:2)
Then stand before the Bema Seat	(II Corinthians 5:10)
Rewarded by the Son.	(II Timothy 4:8)
To place our crowns back at His feet	(Revelation 4:10)
Will be our joy. Our prize most sweet	(Philippians 4:1)
To hear Him say, "Well done."	(Matthew 25:21)
Be seated in the heavenly places	(Ephesians 2:6)
With Christ, forever home.	(Revelation 21:3)
Our walk by faith, and zeal of race,	(II Corinthians 5:6, 7)
Will show the riches of His grace	(II Timothy 4:7)
In ages yet to come.	(Ephesians 2:7)
Come, walk the ancient paths.	(Jeremiah 6:16)

Judy Gerry

Becoming a Follower of Christ

1. Recognize that God loves you:

"For God so loved the world that He gave His one and only Son, that whoever believes in Him shall not perish but have eternal life." (John 3:16)

"But God demonstrates His own love for us in this: While we were still sinners, Christ died for us." (Romans 5:8)

2. Admit that you are a sinner:

"For all have sinned and fall short of the glory of God." (Romans 3:23)

"As it is written: 'There is no one righteous, not even one.'" (Romans 3:10)

3. Recognize Jesus Christ as being God's only remedy for sin:

"For the wages of sin is death, but the gift of God is eternal life in Christ Jesus our Lord." (Romans 6:23)

"Yet all who received Him, to those who believed in His name, He gave the right to become children of God." (John 1:12)

"For what I received I passed on to you as of first importance: that Christ died for our sins according to the Scriptures, that He was buried, that He was raised on the third day according to the Scriptures." (I Corinthians 15:3, 4)

4. Receive Jesus Christ as your personal Savior:

"If you confess with your mouth, 'Jesus is Lord,' and believe in your heart that God raised Him from the dead, you will be saved." (Romans 10:9)

Prayer is simply "talking with God." Right now, go to God in prayer and ask Christ to be your Savior. You might pray something like this:

"Lord Jesus, I need You. I confess that I am a sinner and that You paid the penalty for my sin through Your death on the cross. I believe that You died for my sins and were raised from the dead. I ask You to come into my heart, take control of my life, and make me the kind of person that You want me to be. Thank You for coming into my life as You promised. Amen."

UNIT ONE

WALKING IN CHURCH

"I, therefore, the prisoner of the Lord, entreat you to walk in a manner worthy of the calling with which you have been called, with all humility and gentleness, with patience, showing forbearance to one another in love, being diligent to preserve the unity of the Spirit in the bond of peace."
Ephesians 4:1-3

Unit Chapters:

1. Be Kind - Titus 2:4, 5

2. Be Doers of Good Works - I Timothy 2:9, 10

3. Do Not Be Malicious Gossips - Titus 2:3

4. Receive Instruction with Submissiveness - I Timothy 2:11

5. Older Women Teach and Encourage the Young Women - Titus 2:3, 4; Proverbs 31:26

WALKING IN THE CHURCH AND IN THE WORLD

Before We Begin...
If you are a follower of the Lord Jesus Christ, God calls you a "saint" (I Corinthians 1:2). Every believer is a sanctified member of His church.

Regarding those who have not yet met Christ as their Savior:
Some of you may not yet know Jesus Christ as your personal Savior. This Bible study will be beneficial because any time that God's principles are applied to our lives there will always be a positive result. However, we will never experience God's best in our activities and relationships until we meet Him personally in our own individual lives.

If you have not yet made the wonderful discovery of knowing Christ, please take time to carefully read the preceding page: "Becoming a Follower of Christ." Attempts to live the Christian life without having His power in your life will end in frustration. If you want to experience the abundant life that the Lord has created you to enjoy, before you begin this Bible study, begin to follow Jesus.

Regarding those who already know Jesus Christ as their Savior:
God's Word is clear in delineating that a woman's primary responsibility is found in caring for her husband, children, and home. Yet, the Lord has called Christian women to a high and holy position within the broader scope of functioning within His church. He says that men and women are all "one in Christ Jesus" (Galatians 3:28). Yet, in Scripture the Lord lays out both specific instructions, as well as warnings, for women as they function within His church.

The Lord also directly addresses the issue of Christian women's involvement in the world through their social, community, and political activities.

As we study "Walking in the Church and in the World," open sharing and interaction among women from all walks of life will be essential and valuable. Regardless of our unique, personal circumstances, every woman is a precious creation; a treasure to God Himself (Psalm 83:3).

All of God's Word is for all of us. We need each other; so ***let's get started!***

CHAPTER ONE

BE KIND

Having a heartfelt desire that others experience blessing and joy.

"...encourage the young women... to be kind..."
Titus 2:4, 5

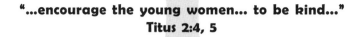

"...encourage the young women... to be kind..."
Titus 2:4, 5

Prayer Points:

Every woman knows that the greatest gift that anyone can give to her is to love and accept those whom she loves. If one wants to do something nice for a mother, be kind to her children. Likewise, if believers want to show their love for the Father, be kind to His children (I John 5:1). All believers call out "Abba! Father!" (Romans 8:15), because we are all brothers and sisters in Christ.

The Lord calls His children to "walk in a manner worthy of the calling with which you have been called" (Ephesians 4:1). Just as it brings parents great joy to see their children loving each other, God the Father delights to see His children loving each other.

The Lord Jesus Christ loves His church. He gave His life for the church and does everything to make her holiness a reality (Ephesians 5:25-27). If believers were "diligent to preserve the unity of the Spirit in the bond of peace," the church would experience terrestrial as well as celestial glory (Ephesians 4:1-3). Yet, sadly, the sentiment expressed in the poem below captures the unfortunate tone found in many churches today:

> *"To live above with saints we love,*
> *oh, that will be such glory;*
> *but to live below with saints we know,*
> *well, that's another story."*

Every believer in the Lord Jesus Christ is a member of His church. Because we are all in His family, the Lord has given specific directives regarding how His children are to walk in the church. God has specifically instructed women to be kind (Titus 2:5).

The fact that society today is suffering from a depletion of kindness is evidenced by the onslaught of bumper stickers exhorting others to "practice random acts of kindness." A symptom of the "last days" will be that men will be "haters of those who do good" (II Timothy 3:3).

As in the early church, a healthy dose of kindness is a welcome commodity. Perhaps today such kindness is even more cherished as its scarcity increases.

Scripture often uses the words "kind" and "good" interchangeably.

Webster's New World College Dictionary defines "kind" this way:

1) *sympathetic, friendly, gentle, tender-hearted, generous, etc.*
2) *cordial (kind regards)*
3) *(Archaic) loving; affectionate*

For purposes of our discussion, one of the dictionary definitions of "good" reads:

1) *morally sound or excellent; specif.,*
   a) *virtuous; honest; just*
   b) *pious; devout*
   c) *kind, benevolent, generous, sympathetic, etc;*
   d) *well-behaved; dutiful*

The Greek word for "kind" used in Titus 2:5 is "agathos." Though "agathos" can also be translated as meaning "good," the nuances of the word are better captured by our English word "kind."

"Agathos" indicates more than being intrinsically good by nature. It describes a moral honor and goodness that is beneficial. Agathos is that inner goodness which makes one capable of doing good. It is a heartfelt desire that others experience blessing and happiness.

Optional: Read Romans 7:18.
Using your concordance and expository dictionary, determine the various meanings of the word "good" in this verse.

What can you determine about the nature of "agathos" and "kalos" from their usage in the text?

**Prayer
Points:**

What do the following verses reveal about God's kindness?

1.　Luke 6:35

2.　Romans 2:4

3.　Titus 3:4-7

It is God's nature to be kind. Man is not intrinsically good and kind. Paul says, "For I know that nothing good dwells in me, that is, in my flesh, for the wishing is present in me, but the doing of the good is not" (Romans 7:18). We need God's kindness to flow through our lives.

As the fruit of the Spirit, it is only through the empowering of the indwelling Holy Spirit that believers can be kind (Galatians 5:22). Our world is thirsting for a touch of kindness today.

Like the lament of David, many are crying out, "There is no one who regards me; there is no escape for me; no one cares for my soul" (Psalm 142:4). Contemporary life is filled with the desperate dirges of women who inwardly moan like Rebekah, "I am tired of living…" (Genesis 27:46).

The Holy Spirit enables believers to possess a kindness unlike any other. He opens the ears of Christians to hear the cries of those in anguish, He opens their eyes to sense others' needs, and He opens their hearts causing them to honestly care for the physical, emotional, mental and spiritual needs of others.

To whom are Christians to be kind and good?

4.　Titus 3:1, 2

5.   Luke 6:35

6.   Galatians 6:10

        To whom are Christians to be especially kind?

7.   Romans 12:9, 10

8.   Psalm 133:1

God's Word exhorts believers to be kind to each other. While giving mental assent to that "general" truth, and even truly desiring to be a kind woman, it can be challenging to actually follow through when faced with "specifics." Are there any "specific" believers toward whom you find it difficult to be genuinely kind?

Only the grace of God and the power of His Holy Spirit can provide that inner disposition to genuinely seek the best for others (Romans 15:5-7). Women of God must be on guard not to let deceitful charm give the appearance of kindness while not sincerely being kind at heart (Proverbs 31:30). "Let love be without hypocrisy" (Romans 12:9). Don't just pretend to love others; really love them!

But what are we to do if we find ourselves actually disliking another believer? How can a woman have "the teaching of kindness...on her tongue" (Proverbs 31:26) when there is even slight resentment in her heart?

1.   *We must forgive those who have offended us.*

It may be difficult to be kind toward one who has offended either you or someone whom you love. According to the following verses, what may be necessary in order to genuinely become a kind and tenderhearted woman?

9.	Ephesians 4:31, 32

Prayer Points:

10.	Colossians 3:12, 13

God warns against allowing a root of bitterness to spring up in our hearts. Unchecked resentment will grow, causing trouble, and hurting many in their spiritual lives (Hebrews 12:15).

- Is there anyone against whom you are holding a grudge?

- What steps do you need to take?

- When will you take that action?

	(Specific steps involved in reconciliation will be covered in Chapter Three.)

**II.	We need to understand and appreciate our differences.**

Occasionally, there may be people toward whom we find it difficult to demonstrate kindness because they are so different from ourselves. The development of kindness toward others may be stymied when we fail to understand the purpose behind our differences.

The Lord has intentionally designed the church to be comprised of many diverse types of individuals. He tells us that there is a direct parallel between the way that an actual human body functions and the way that the Body of Christ works. Just as the various components of the physical body have similarities and differences, each unique individual in the Body of Christ has similarities and differences. Read the verses below: Note what believers have in common, and note their differences.

	Scriptures	Believers Share in Common	Differences Between Believers
11.	Romans 12:4, 5		
12.	Ephesians 4:15, 16		
13.	I Corinthians 12:12-27		

Prayer Points:

What part of the body do you sense that you may be?

Why do you think that you are that part?

Do you ever feel unimportant in the body? What does God say about that?

Do you ever feel competitive with another part of the body? What does God say about that?

According to verse 26, how are we to respond to the pains or joys of other believers?

Relate a recent experience when you sincerely suffered with another believer as you sensed his pain.

Relate a recent experience when you sincerely rejoiced with another believer's success.

Prayer Points:

The above analogy comparing the Body of Christ to the human body is sandwiched between two portions of Scripture related to spiritual gifts (I Corinthians 12:1-11, 28-31). Differences related to each believer's function within the Body can result in misunderstanding among believers.

· A woman with the gift of teaching may wonder why another is not spending hours in study each day (Romans 12:7). That teacher may not realize that the other woman is exercising her gift of helps and has been busy serving others unnoticed (Romans 16:12).

· Another sister in the Lord may be devoted to a ministry of prayer (I Timothy 5:5). She may have difficulty understanding why the evangelists are not at home on their knees day and night.

· One with the gift of mercy may think that the woman with the gift of exhortation "comes on too strong," while the exhorter sees the merciful one as "wishy-washy."

We must accept one another because together we are bringing glory to God (Romans 15:5-7).

Care must also be taken not to covet another's spiritual gifts or talents within the body. We are all one body; we are all essential. Certain types of gifts may evoke more public acclaim, however, the Lord has said that those who serve seen only by God will be rewarded openly by Him (Matthew 6:3-6).

Optional: For further study on spiritual gifts you may do a topical study using your concordance and expository dictionary. A parallel text to I Corinthians 12 is Romans 12:3-8.

Also see I Corinthians 1:4-7; I Timothy 4:14, 15, and II Timothy 1:6.

According to the following verses, what is the purpose of the different spiritual gifts given within the church?

14.   I Corinthians 12:7

15.   I Corinthians 14:26

16.   I Peter 4:10, 11

Immediately after citing the various spiritual gifts given uniquely to each believer, Paul explains that showing love toward each other far exceeds gifts in importance. Love is to be the motivating factor in all that believers do. He carefully notes that love is kind (I Corinthians 13:4).

John repeats many times that the believer's main call is to love one another (I John 3:11, 23; 4:7, 11, 12). This love is to be continually increasing (Philippians 1:9-11; I Thessalonians 4:9, 10).

In the Scriptures below, note the benefits resulting from our obedience to God's command to love each other.

17.   I John 3:14

18.   John 13:34, 35

19.   John 17:20-23

        What has Jesus given to us to enable us to love each other?

20.   Romans 15:5-7

**Prayer
Points:**

It is God's will that believing women be kind, especially to others in His church. Kindness is that inner disposition that causes us to sincerely desire the best for others. We are to "regard one another as more important" than ourselves (Philippians 2:3).

An alarm should sound in our hearts when we notice that we do not want to be kind toward another. If we are not kind toward another, we are unkind. One may argue that it is possible to love another believer while refraining from being kind. Does refraining from being kind constitute unkindness? What does God say?

21.   Proverbs 27:5

Is there some believer toward whom, though you are not openly hostile, yet you do not overtly demonstrate kindness? What should you do about this?

When the "kindness alarm" rings in our hearts, we should immediately take it to the Lord and ask Him to reveal the root of our problem.

- If it is a lack of forgiveness, we are to forgive that person.

- If another's personality "grates" against us, we are to patiently bear with them (Colossians 3:12, 13; I Corinthians 13:4).

- If we are jealous of another, we are to repent (James 3:14-16). Unkindness is disobedience. Disobedience is sin.

Others may never change, but we can be changed. We can appropriate a kind heart from the One Who is kindness Himself, Jesus Christ (Ephesians 2:7).

There are those who do not hear any "kindness alarm" due to their insensitive natures. If you find yourself in this category, begin asking the Lord to show you how to be kind to others so that you can show Him love. Be alert to opportunities to be kind. Ask God to open your ears, your eyes, and your heart.

"To sum up, let all be harmonious, sympathetic, brotherly, kindhearted, and humble in spirit; not returning evil for evil, or insult for insult, but giving a blessing instead; for you were called for the very purpose that you might inherit a blessing" (I Peter 3:8, 9).

Take a moment and note below any area(s) in which the Holy Spirit has convicted you during today's study.

What steps do you intend on taking this week to **"put on kindness"** (Colossians 3:12, 13)?

Prayer Points:

SUMMARY:

Define being "kind" in your own terms. You could use a synonym, a motto, a poem or a prayer, or even make a drawing to show your understanding of this quality.

DISCUSSION:

Tell about a recent experience when someone was kind toward you. What effect did that kindness have on you?

APPLICATION:

A Christian women's group leader is faced with a problem. A new member of the group is irritating other women due to her abrasive personality. She doesn't fit the social status of the other ladies who are feeling increasingly uncomfortable with her presence. How would you advise this group leader to deal with this situation?

CHAPTER TWO

BE DOERS OF GOOD WORKS

Putting into action my desire
to see others experience blessing and joy.

"Likewise, I want women to adorn themselves with proper clothing, modestly and discreetly, not with braided hair and gold or pearls or costly garments; but rather by means of good works, as befits women making a claim to godliness."
I Timothy 2:9, 10

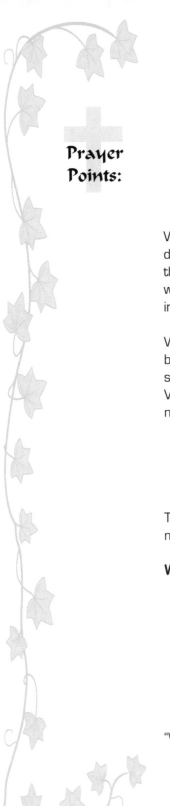

**Prayer
Points:**

**"Likewise, I want women to adorn themselves with
proper clothing, modestly and discreetly,
not with braided hair and gold or pearls or costly garments;
but rather by means of good works,
as befits women making a claim to godliness."
I Timothy 2:9, 10**

While kindness is the inner disposition that causes one to sincerely desire the best for another, good works are those actions that make the desire become a reality. Kindness is the good intention; good works put feet and hands to that intention. Good works are kindness in action.

When the subject of "doing good works" comes up, many women become gripped with fear and panic. Images of volunteer sign-up sheets circulating around the room whirl through the imagination. Visions of harried women tethered by ball and chain to the church nursery abound.

What is your feeling, or attitude, as we delve into the topic of women being doers of good works?

The term "good works" is a combination of two Greek words; "agathos" meaning kind or good, plus "ergon" meaning work or task.

Webster's New World College Dictionary defines "good" this way:

> 1) morally sound or excellent; specifically:
> a) virtuous;
> b) pious;
> c) kind, benevolent, generous, sympathetic, etc;
> d) well-behaved; dutiful,
> e) proper; becoming - as good manners.

"Work" is defined as being:

> 1) physical or mental effort exerted to do or make something;
> a.) purposeful activity;
> b.) labor;
> c.) toil

God Himself is the ultimate example of "being a Doer of good works." The Lord's kind intention toward us (Ephesians 1:5) manifested itself by taking action. "For God so loved the world, that He gave His only begotten Son...." (John 3:16).

Christ came to earth to serve those whom He loves (Matthew 20:28). Scripture tells us that He took on the nature of a servant (Philippians 2:7) and "He went about doing good" (Acts 10:38).

Prayer Points:

Real love affects real life; viable affection is evidenced by visible action.

What we "do" as believers is the outward manifestation of our inward hearts. Living faith will always affect life actions (James 2:20-22). Each day in the life of a believer provides opportunities to be "doers of good works." Yet, it is apparent that within the Body of Christ there are three basic types of responses to the Lord's command to do good works.

There exists in the body a large group of women who exhibit limited good works. They are "artful dodgers" when it comes to evading most commitments to others. These women will not say "yes." They are **rusting out.**

There is a second group of women who have overburdened themselves with good deeds; feeling obligated to accept every opportunity for service put before them. They cannot say "no." These women often complain that they are **burning out**.

A third group of women has an accurate biblical grasp of what it means to be a doer of good works. Relying on God's strength to flow through them, they are setting aside their personal comfort as they make themselves available for God's use. These women have learned to say "wait" as they seek His will. They are being **cleaned out** as channels through which God's love can flow.

Of the three groups mentioned above, which one best describes your life?

RUSTING OUT

A woman's inaccurate perspective of God's purpose for her life may result in missed opportunities. Women who avoid participating in

good works often are unaware of the importance that God places on serving others and using their time wisely (Ephesians 5:15, 16).

What do the following verses reveal about doing good works?

Prayer Points:

1.　　Ephesians 2:8-10

Optional: Using your Greek dictionary, look up the meaning of the word "workmanship" in Ephesians 2:10. Note any additional insight that this definition provides regarding how God wants to use your life.

2.　　Titus 3:5, 8

3.　　Colossians 3:23, 24

4.　　I Corinthians 3:10-15

Though our salvation is not dependent upon doing good deeds, our good works are a demonstration of the faith that we have (Titus 1:16). According to the above verses, is there any benefit to doing good, aside from our own personal sense of satisfaction?

Scripture admonishes women in the church to adorn themselves with good works, rather than with elaborate hairstyles, gold, pearls, or expensive garments (I Timothy 2:9, 10). Believers are the bride of Christ (Ephesians 5:31, 32). What do the following verses reveal about the clothing of the bride of Christ at the future marriage feast in heaven?

5.　　Revelation 19:7, 8

What comprises the "fabric" of the bride's wedding gown?

In light of these verses, if the wedding dresses were given out today, describe what yours might look like.

What would you like for your dress to look like?

There are many who, though filled with good intentions, are rusting out due to lack of follow-through. "There's many a slip 'twixt the cup and the lip," and often the inner motivation of kindness is short-circuited, never coming to fruition in good deeds.

The Lord exhorts us to love each other not only with words, but also with actual deeds (I John 3:18). He also warns believers to follow through on commitments so that we may not fall under judgment (James 5:12; II Corinthians 9:7).

How sad for the woman who chooses to rust out, neglecting the opportunities that God has set before her. She is missing much of the beauty and fulfillment that the Lord has for her in this life, and the reward in the life to come.

BURNING OUT

Since the Lord says that His yoke is easy and His burden is light, why do so many people seem to be straining under the heavy load of serving Christ (Matthew 11:30)?

Much like the motor of a kitchen hand-mixer which burns out when given a task for which it is not designed, women may assume tasks for which they are not designed (Ephesians 2:10). We always have time to do what God wants us to do. It has been said that if we have too much to do, then we are doing too much.

There are several reasons why so many Christian women are suffering from burn out today.

Prayer Points:

Misplaced Priorities:

Burn out may occur when one has misplaced priorities that sap one's strength and time. When a woman's priorities are aligned with her Creator's, she will not fall prey to the tyranny of the urgent, or impulsively respond to needs for which she was not designed. Reacting to every apparent need without prayer may actually hinder God's work (John 18:11).

We need to seek discernment as we meet others' needs. For example, though we are to feed the hungry, perhaps the Lord may be using their hunger to teach them to work (II Thessalonians 3:10). Though we are to be kind, friendly and welcoming to all, we are to shun false teachers (II John 10, 11). Perhaps the prodigal son may not have returned home if others, lacking discernment, had met his apparent physical needs (Luke 15:11-32).

6.   Romans 14:23

        Can doing good works ever be sin?

Lack of Personal Organization:

Burn out may result from a lack of personal organization in life. What does the following text reveal about the nature of burn out, and possible solutions to the problem?

7.   Numbers 11:10-15

Moses certainly suffered "burn out after the burning bush!" He became overwhelmed by the problems and bad attitudes of others. He expected too much of himself by misunderstanding his assignment, and assumed responsibilities that were God's alone (11:12). Moses had forgotten that his "responsibility" was to "respond" to God's "ability" to work through Him. This led him into personal depression and the desire to die.

8.   Numbers 11:16, 17

What steps did the Lord instruct Moses to take in order to combat burn out?

Wrong Motives in Serving:

Burn out may result from having the wrong motives in serving. Each woman should ask herself why she desires to do the good deeds in which she is involved. Perhaps she is motivated by a desire to be praised by others, by a need to be needed, perhaps outside activities provide an acceptable escape from the responsibilities of her home, or she may be motivated by sheer guilt.

What do the following Scriptures say regarding motives in life?

9.   I Corinthians 10:31

10.   Colossians 3:17

Impure motives can lead to frustration and disappointment in serving others. How would you assess your own motives?

> **"For this is the love of God, that we keep His commandments; and His commandments are not burdensome."**
> **I John 5:3**

How sad for the woman who feels burned out in doing good deeds. She is missing much of the joy and power that the Lord has for her in this life.

CLEANED OUT

Women who desire to be used by the Lord in order to bring Him glory must have pure motives. Since the heart is incredibly deceitful, discerning our own motives for serving is impossible (Jeremiah 17:9, 10). Like David, each must pray, "Search me, O God, and know my heart; try me and know my thoughts; and see if there be any hurtful way in me" (Psalm 139:23, 24).

Prayer Points:

Prayer Points:

When the Lord reveals impure motives or sin in one's life, repentance is necessary. We must be cleaned out in order for the Holy Spirit to have full control of our lives. All self-will, personal desires, and hidden agendas must be scoured from our hearts.

How is one prepared for good works?

11.   II Timothy 2:21

12.   II Timothy 3:16, 17

13.   Titus 3:14

Believers are to be "an example of good deeds" [Titus 2:7]. What is the origin of power to do good works?

14.   II Corinthians 9:8

        Does this verse reveal anything related to "burning out"?

15.   Hebrews 13:20, 21

What should be our attitude regarding doing good works?

16.   Titus 2:14

17.   Titus 3:1

18.   II Corinthians 9:7

19.   Romans 12:11

20.   I Peter 4:9

After we are cleansed from any impediment which would hinder the work of the Lord through our lives, when our motives are right before God, and we are able to serve with a holy attitude, then we are ready to do the good works which God has prepared for us to do.

In what specific activities does the Lord want His people to be involved? Scripture is quite specific about the good works that God desires to see in His church. There are also specific directives related to the good deeds that He loves to see in believing women.

Sharing and Giving:

> *"The act of making one's resources available to another.
> It may include freely turning over the possession or control to another."*

The following passages reveal some of the types of good works that the Lord desires to see in His church. The verses related specifically to women are in bold type.

Read:

Hebrews 13:16	Romans 12:13	II Corinthians 8:3
II Corinthians 9:13	I Timothy 6:18	Acts 4:32
Luke 6:35	**Luke 8:1-3**	I John 3:17

Do you notice and take advantage of opportunities to share your resources with others? Excluding your weekly tithes, when was the last time that you shared or gave of your material resources to another?

Sharing and giving may apply to more than one's material possessions. What other "commodities" might a woman share, or give, to another?

How would you rate yourself in the area of sharing and giving?

Prayer Points:

Hospitality:

"The act, quality, or practice of being friendly and loving to strangers and guests"

Romans 12:13   Hebrews 13:1, 2   I Timothy 3:2
I Timothy 5:10   Titus 1:8   I Peter 4:9
Acts 16:13-15, 40 **Acts 18:1-3**   **II Kings 4:8-11**

Do you notice and greet strangers, making them feel welcome and valued?

In groups of believers, do you find yourself chatting solely with your old friends, or do you make an overt effort to welcome newcomers?

Do you make an equal effort to welcome those who may not be "socially acceptable" in your group? (James 2:2-9)

Do you make your home available as a forum for hospitality?

How would you rate yourself in the area of Hospitality?

Showing Affection and Honor:

"To exhibit a fond or tender feeling that conveys high regard and respect."

Romans 12:10   Romans 16:16   I Corinthians 16:20
II Corinthians 13:12 I Peter 5:14   **Matthew 26:6-12**

A "holy kiss" was a token of Christian brotherhood, or sisterhood, which took place between persons of the same sex.

What types of actions might convey a similar meaning in contemporary culture?

How would you rate yourself in the area of showing affection and honor?

Assisting Those In Distress:

"Helping those who have a need, imposed either by external circumstances, or by inward pressure."

Prayer Points:

Prisoners	Hebrews 13:3
Meeting physical needs of the poor	James 2:15, 16
	Proverbs 31:20
	I Timothy 5:10
Widows	**Acts 9:39**
	Isaiah 1:17
Fatherless, orphans	James 1:27
	Psalm 82:3
Foreigners	Deuteronomy 14:29

Do you readily hear the silent cries of those in need?

When was the last time that you participated in assisting the physical needs of one in distress?

When was the last time that you assisted meeting the emotional needs of another in distress?

How would you rate yourself in the area of assisting those in distress?

Building Up One Another:

"Promoting the spiritual growth of another."

Through praying -   James 5:16   **I Timothy 5:5**
                      Acts 1:14   **Acts12:12**
                      Romans 12:12

Through caring for the weaker brother -   Romans 14:13, 19

Through comforting one another -   I Thessalonians 4:18
                                        Romans 12:15

Prayer Points:

Through encouraging one another -

I Thessalonians 5:11
Hebrews 3:13; 10:25
Acts 20:31, 31
Isaiah 41:6

How would you rate yourself in the area of building up one another?

Serving In General:

"The outward manifestation of believers in presenting their bodies to God as a living sacrifice, to be used as He desires."

Galatians 5:13   Romans 16:1, 2   I Peter 1:22
I John 3:16   **Mark 15:40, 41**   **I Timothy 5:10**

Would you say that you are sensitive to the needs of others?

Would you say that you are available to help meet others' needs?

How do you regularly help to meet the needs of others?

It is essential to note that a woman's primary area of ministry and good works is in her own home. Paul gives a list of good works that should be manifested by a godly widow. The first "good work" mentioned is that "she has brought up children" (I Timothy 5:9, 10).

Unfortunately, there are women who find it easier to serve others than to serve their own families. Some would rather participate in a church cleaning day than iron their own husband's shirts. There are women who will bake elegant edibles for the ladies' Bible study, whose children must forage for their own food at dinnertime. While cheerfully ministering to the elderly at church, there are some women who would never invite their mother-in-laws for the evening. What does God say?

21.   I Timothy 5:8

22.   I Timothy 5:16

Scripture gives us the example of Dorcas as a "woman who was abounding with deeds of kindness and charity, which she continually did." Read the following passage and note any insights regarding a woman who does good deeds.

23.   Acts 9:36-42

How does the Lord Jesus view kindnesses that are extended toward those whom He loves?

24.   Matthew 25:40

Don't rust out.   The Lord has called each of us to fulfill specific roles in life. We were created for good works which God prepared uniquely for us before the foundation of the world (Ephesians 1:4; 2:10). Our greatest fulfillment in life will come from obediently allowing the Holy Spirit to accomplish His work through us.

Don't burn out. Ask God today that as He makes you sensitive to the needs of others, that He will specifically direct you in your response to those needs. After doing the good works in our own homes, we should ask the Father what He would like for us to accomplish for His other children.

Be cleaned out. Become a vessel useful to the Master, prepared for every good work. Putting aside self-will and personal desires, obey the Lord with pure motives and a happy heart.

> **"And let us not lose heart in doing good,
> for in due time we shall reap if we do not grow weary.
> So then, while we have opportunity, let us do good to all
> men, and especially to those who are of the
> household of the faith."
> Galatians 6:9, 10**

Prayer Points:

SUMMARY:

Define "doing good works" in your own terms. You could use a synonym, a motto, a poem or a prayer, or even make a drawing to show your understanding of this concept.

DISCUSSION:

Hebrews 10:24 exhorts believers to consider how to "stimulate one another to love and good deeds." Getting practical, how do we go about motivating each other in this way?

APPLICATION:

A young Christian woman breaks down in tears at a committee meeting explaining that she is suffering from "burn out." What counsel can you give her?

CHAPTER THREE

DO NOT BE MALICIOUS GOSSIPS

*Speaking the truth in such a way
as to always present others in the best possible light.*

NO!

**"Older women likewise are to be reverent
in their behavior, not malicious gossips..."
Titus 2:3**

Walking in the Church and in the World

**"Older women likewise are to be reverent
in their behavior, not malicious gossips..."
Titus 2:3**

Prayer Points:

The doctor who asks a patient to stick out his tongue realizes that the appearance of the tongue can indicate much about one's physical condition. In much the same way, an examination of our tongue reveals much about our spiritual health.

God tells us that "death and life are in the power of the tongue" (Proverbs 18:21). Why does God's Word make such a big deal about something as tiny as the tongue?

The Lord tells us that the tongue is small but powerful. In the same way that a horse's bit can direct the entire animal, and a ship's rudder can determine the direction of a vessel, the tongue is a spark that can set on fire the course of our life (James 3:3-6).

The childhood adage "sticks and stones may break my bones, but names will never hurt me" couldn't be more erroneous. Words can indeed hurt. The Lord clearly warns us of the deadly nature of the human tongue. He tells us that the tongue is an untamable, potent force. It is a "restless evil and full of deadly poison" (James 3:8). The vocal nature of natural man is described as "an open grave, with their tongues they keep deceiving, the poison of asps is under their lips" (Romans 3:13).

One's words speak volumes about the character of the one speaking (Proverbs 17:7). Older Christian women, as well as those women who are in leadership, are examples of godliness to others. They are particularly exhorted to guard their speech and refrain from being malicious gossips (Titus 2:3; I Timothy 3:11).

Webster's New World College Dictionary defines "gossip"in this way:

1.)   a) godparent
      b) a close friend
2.)   a) a person who chatters or repeats idle talk and rumors, esp. about
         the private affairs of others
3.)   a) such talk or rumors
      b) chatter

"Malicious" is defined as:

having, showing, or caused by malice; spiteful; intentionally mischievous or harmful

When the Lord instructs women to "not be malicious gossips," the implication is that our speech should never be motivated by any evil intent to hurt another person. Godly women are not to slander others, to falsely accuse another, or to say anything harboring ill will.

It is interesting to note that an increase in malicious gossiping is a defining factor of the difficult times indicative of the "last days" (II Timothy 3:3).

Prayer Points:

Optional: Look up the Greek word for "malicious" used in Titus 2:3, I Timothy 3:11, and II Timothy 3:3.

What is the literal interpretation of this Greek word?

Of whom is this word used as a title in Scripture? (See John 8:44)

What English word(s) come from this root?

The words that we use are more potent than we often realize. What insights regarding the power of the tongue can you glean from the following verses?

1. Proverbs 15:4

2. Proverbs 18:8

3. Proverbs 23:16

Prayer Points:

4.   Proverbs 10:11

What damaging effects can the tongue cause?

5.   Proverbs 11:9

6.   Proverbs 16:27, 28

7.   Proverbs 17:9

8.   Proverbs 25:23

9.   Proverbs 26:17

10.   Proverbs 26:20

While acknowledging that the tongue is a "weak area" in their lives, many maintain that they are "strong Christians" in spite of that weakness. What does God tell us about the correlation between controlling the tongue and one's spiritual life?

11.   James 1:26

Though Satan himself is the father of all lies, we must take personal responsibility for any sin that we have committed. The deep-seated sins of the tongue are not merely superficial and to be taken lightly.

What do the following texts reveal?

12.   Matthew 12:34 (Luke 6:45)

Prayer Points:

13.   Matthew 15:18 (Mark 7:20-22)

The tongue is like a gauge on a car dashboard. The red light is an indication that there is trouble inside, under the hood. Similarly, our tongue indicates the spiritual health of our heart. Trouble with the tongue is an indication that we must look "under the hood" in order to deal with the source of the problem- our heart.

Just as Adam and Eve tried to hide from God after they sinned, it is human nature to try and hide from our Father when we sin. What does His Word say?

14.   Luke 12:2, 3

15.   Matthew 12:36, 37

After God confronted Adam and Eve with their sin, each of them attempted to rationalize and justify their wrong actions. When confronted with sins of the tongue, such as gossip, lying, or slander, we often attempt to justify our sin.

What does God say about a person who claims that her words were only meant as a joke?

16.   Proverbs 26:18, 19

What if the information given regarding another person is indeed accurate? One may attempt to justify her sin of gossip by pointing out that she was only telling the truth. What does God say?

17.   Ephesians 4:15

18.   Proverbs 16:2

19.   I Peter 4:8

20.   Proverbs 19:11

Is it possible to say the right thing at the wrong time? Is that a sin?

21.   Proverbs 25:20

22.   Proverbs 27:14

23.   Proverbs 15:23

24.   Proverbs 25:11

Though "holding your tongue" is usually a good idea (Proverbs 17:28), is there ever an occasion when silence can be a sin?

25.   Proverbs 10:18

26.   Proverbs 27:5

Everyone has committed sins of the tongue (James 3:2). The varieties of such sins are innumerable. We are all guilty and will be held accountable for every idle word that we speak while on earth. God hates sin and we cannot please Him when we continue to justify and defend ourselves.

As you read the above passages, was there any area in which the Holy Spirit convicted you of personal sins of the tongue? Are you willing to confess that sin and repent, turn from, that sin?

God's Word gives us direction on how to avoid getting caught in the "mouth-trap." What can you learn from the following?

27.   Proverbs 2:3-5

28.   Proverbs 6:2, 3

29.   Proverbs 10:19

30.   Proverbs 15:1

31.   Proverbs 15:28

32.   Proverbs 17:4

**Prayer
Points:**

33.   Proverbs 18:13

34.   Proverbs 28:13

35.   Ephesians 4:29

36.   Colossians 3:8, 9

Before speaking, one should ask: "Is what I am going to say *true*?" "Is what I am going to say *good*?" "Is what I am going to say *necessary*?"

One may argue that there is a big difference between inadvertently saying something at the wrong time and in being a malicious gossip. Some sins of the tongue do not harbor ill will, while malicious gossiping is intentionally harmful.

Spitefully speaking is deadly. Many homes, marriages, friendships, entire churches, and even nations have been destroyed due to the toxic tongue.

What would cause women to become malicious gossips? Quite simply, one person holds a grudge against another. Following his description of the sins of the tongue, James concludes by saying,

> **"...where jealousy and selfish ambition exist,
> there is disorder and every evil thing"
> James 3:16.**

God tells us that anger and wrath are fierce, but that even they are not as strong as the power of jealousy (Proverbs 27:4). The spark igniting spiteful speech can very often be traced to the sins of jealousy and selfish ambition.

Perhaps this is true in your own life. Think of a person with whom you have either subtle, or overt, tension.

❧   Are you jealous of that person in some way?

Do you even slightly resent that the other person has it better than you do? Do you sincerely rejoice in the successes that they experience with their ...

☐   Family, children, husband?
☐   Physical attributes or talents?
☐   Good reputation or accomplishments?
☐   Ministry opportunities?
☐   Material assets?
☐   Lifestyle?
☐   Spiritual maturity or their walk with the Lord?

❧   Does your own selfish ambition dig in its heels and set a wall between you?

Does your speech subtly hint that you may say things about others because ...

☐   You want yourself to be perceived as a little better than the other person?
☐   You want others to know that person being discussed is "not so hot"; that they're not as great as everyone seems to think?
☐   You are jockeying to replace the other person's status or responsibility?
☐   You want everyone to know that you're so important that you have the "inside scoop" on another's life?

Beware! This is serious business. It is imperative that we take care to guard our hearts with all diligence so that such sin will not take root (Proverbs 4:23). Many will be hurt if we refuse to immediately deal with our bitter sin when the Holy Spirit reveals it to us (Hebrews 12:15). We must take every thought captive (II Corinthians 10:5), and saturate our hearts and minds with things that please God (Psalm 119:11; Philippians 4:8).

Evidently, the early church faced the problem of strife between women. Euodia and Syntyche are named specifically as having a "personality clash." Though they are remembered as good Christian women, how sad that these women are also remembered for all posterity in God's eternal Word for their inability to get along (Philippians 4:2, 3).

Prayer Points:

Prayer Points:

How will you be remembered by those who know you? Often those who know us best can detect areas of ill will in our hearts which we are unable, or unwilling, to admit. Our hearts are so deceitful that we can even fool ourselves (Jeremiah 17:9). Ask your family if they have noticed any area, or individuals, against whom you harbor ill. Such sin may not show up as overt ugliness; rather, it may be evidenced by a lack of overt kindness.

When the Lord reveals the hidden sin that spawns malicious gossip, we must confess and repent of that sin. Rather than holding onto ugly attitudes nesting in our hearts, we are to forgive others from our hearts because Christ has forgiven us (Matthew 18:21-35; Colossians 3:13).

The moment that we participate in malicious gossip, our sin has become no longer hidden. It has been publicly spewed forth like venom, poisoning others. Those hearing our words have been infected, and the reputation of the one slandered has been wounded.

What does Scripture instruct us to do?

37.   James 5:16

Is there anyone to whom you must confess your sin, and from whom you need to ask forgiveness? (A word of caution: "confession" done in the wrong way can amplify damage already done. For additional counsel see "When Confessing Our Sins of the Tongue to Others" located at the end of this chapter.)

Public confession to offended parties is a humbling experience, which is tempting to avoid. One may convince herself that what she said "wasn't that big of a deal," that the other person probably didn't even notice, and that God has already forgiven her. What does Jesus say?

38.   Matthew 5:23, 24

Have you ever obediently applied this verse to your life? What was the result?

God will give grace to those who humble themselves through confession and reconciliation (James 4:6-10). He will bless us and come near to us. One additional benefit to such obedience is that the pain involved in humbling ourselves acts as a powerful deterrent to future verbal sin!

Prayer Points:

There are occasions when a believer overtly sins, either intentionally or unintentionally, against another. The guilty party may not attempt reconciliation through confession. What is the offended party to do in such a situation?

Some wrongfully deal with their pain by gossiping to others about how they were offended. Rather than talking with others about the offense, one should take her pain to the Lord Himself. It may then even be necessary for the one offended to gently approach the guilty party personally. After getting the facts straight, and being committed to loving forgiveness, what does the Lord instruct us to do?

39.   Matthew 18:15-17

Have you ever obediently applied this verse to your life? What was the result?

Correctly following the steps of confession, forgiveness and reconciliation requires the grace and mercy of God. The benefits, however, make it well worth the effort.

One reward of restraining the tongue is that the "present is pleasant." There are immediate blessings:

40.   I Peter 3:8-12

        What are the rewards of guarding the tongue?

***When we follow the Lord's direction regarding the tongue and gossip
we may be blessed by gaining a friend.***

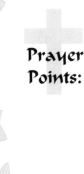

Prayer Points:

Rebuke one another:
> *"Blessed are friends who set you right when you get off the track;*
> *friends who tell you to your face and not behind your back."*
> [See Matthew 18:15-17]

Forgive one another:
> *"Blessed are friends who see your faults and know you're an*
> *'unfinished' saint; They forgive and like you for yourself,*
> *forgetting what you 'ain't!'"*
> [See II Corinthians 2:6-8]

Restore one another:
> *"Blessed are friends who really like to see your problems patched;*
> *And welcome you back with open arms*
> *without any strings attached!"*
> [see Galatians 6:1]

A second benefit of bridling the tongue is that we are a blessing to those around us. Our words are "sweet to the soul and healing to the bones" as they are a "fountain of life" (Proverbs 16:24; 10:11).

The greatest reward of mastering the mouth is that it delights our Father (Proverbs 12:22).

41.   Prayerfully write out Psalm 19:12-14.

Is there any area of your life that you need to confess or change as a result of studying today's lesson?

If so, what are you trusting the Holy Spirit to change in you?

When are you going to begin cooperating with the Lord in making those changes?

> **"Set a guard, O Lord, over my mouth,**
> **keep watch over the door of my lips."**
> **Psalms 141:3**

WHEN CONFESSING OUR SINS OF THE TONGUE TO OTHERS

Prayer Points:

1. Resist the temptation to deal with the surface issue; ask the Lord to reveal to you the root of your heart problem. Any time that we get defensive, or if we become angry with others, the root problem usually lies in our personal pride. Remember, the problem that we see in others is most likely the root of the problem in our own hearts.

2. Confess the sin of your own heart rather than revisiting the details of the specific situation. If we "confess" by rekindling the specific details of a disagreement, we may re-ignite the pain.

Example:
Do say: "Janet, please forgive me. I had an arrogant and proud attitude when we were talking this morning. I was wrong."

Do NOT say: "Janet, when you started bragging about how your children were better behaved than mine, I responded wrongly. I should never have tried to tell you that everyone thinks that your children are out of control. I'm sorry."

3. Make sure that you are dealing only with those who are actually offended. Resist the temptation to spread more gossip by bringing new participants into the circle of offense.

Example:
Do NOT say: "Betty, please pray for me. I am going to confess to Susie that I told the ladies' Bible study how jealous she is of my beautiful new home."

4. Assume 100% of the blame for your personal sins. Do not use the "confession" as an opportunity to "convict" the one whom you have offended. Do not implicate the sin in another person; speak only of your own!

Example:
Do say: "Sherry, I am sorry that I was angry yesterday when we were talking. There is no excuse for my arrogant and rude behavior. Will you please forgive me?"

Do NOT say: "Sherry, I am sorry that I reacted in anger yesterday when you spoke to me with such harsh words. Your insensitivity threw me over the edge."

Prayer Points:

5. Acknowledge that your actions caused pain.

Example:

Do say: "Kathy, I'm so sorry for the way that I hurt you in front of the Bible class. My words were abrasive and arrogant. The Lord is showing me that I have a real problem with my proud heart. I sinned, and I hurt you. Please forgive me."

Do NOT say: "Kathy, 'IF' what I said in front of the class hurt you, well, I'm sorry."

6. Do not use your "confession" as an opportunity to explain, justify, or defend your own sin.

Example:

Do say: "Bill, I am sorry for the ugly things that I said last night. It makes me sad to realize how selfish I am, and I know that my attitude grieves the Lord. Please forgive me."

Do NOT say: "Bill, I am sorry that I said ugly things about your family last night. I've really been tired lately, and I was just frustrated with all of the constant, unrealistic demands that people have been placing on me."

7. Ask those whom you have offended to forgive you. Simply saying that you are sorry about the offense does not comprise a confession; asking them to forgive you opens the door for a restored relationship.

Example:

Do say: "Carrie, I am so sorry that I betrayed our friendship by telling Marie what you had shared with me in confidence. I was wrong. Will you please forgive me?"

Do NOT say: "Carrie, I am sorry that you got upset when I told Marie what you had shared with me."

SUMMARY:

Define "not being a malicious gossip" in your own terms. You could use a synonym, a motto, a poem or a prayer, or even make a drawing to show your understanding of this quality.

Prayer Points:

DISCUSSION:

Have you ever seen a situation where malicious gossiping caused harm in the church? How could that situation have been handled better biblically?

APPLICATION:

Your teenage daughter has a group of Christian friends whose conversations tend to gravitate toward malicious gossip. Your daughter asks for advice regarding how to encourage the group to stop gossiping. What is your advice?

CHAPTER FOUR

Receive Instruction with Submissiveness

*Trusting the Holy Spirit to teach me
through those in authority during public worship.*

**"Let a woman quietly receive instruction
with entire submissiveness."
I Timothy 2:11**

**"Let a woman quietly receive instruction
with entire submissiveness."
I Timothy 2:11**

**Prayer
Points:**

Women and men are equals. They are co-heirs of the grace of life (I Peter 3:7). As children of God through faith in Christ Jesus, "there is neither male nor female; for you are all one in Christ Jesus" (Galatians 3:28). The Creator of both male and female regards them as spiritually equal.

Men and women are equal. But men and women are not the same.

Though men and women share the same distinct relationship with Christ, they are delegated differing roles in His church. Though they have a common calling, they have diverse ministerial mandates. With equal standing and status, they have differing domains of duty and scopes of service. While participating in a shared definite purpose in God's plan, men and women are assigned different places in God's plan.

The Creator designed men and women to fulfill different functions.

Many casual readers of the Bible erroneously assume that the men who penned the holy Scriptures had something against women. Prior to the advent of Christianity women were treated as chattel. They were viewed as having little value and they had few, if any, rights. The revolutionary writings of Scripture placed women on equal par with men. The teachings of Christ have done more to honor and elevate women than any other factor in history. The Lord loves women, after He created them He called His creation "very good" (Genesis 1:31)!

God's creation is replete with examples of how various parts of a given system work together for the benefit of that system. Such order can be seen in the grand planetary scheme of the universe, in the example of instruments playing in an orchestra, as well as being demonstrated by the interworking organs of the human body. Various components, functioning in differing roles, effectively work together to harmoniously accomplish a set goal. There is great order evidenced in creation.

"God is not a God of confusion" and He desires that "all things be done properly and in an orderly manner" (I Corinthians 14:33, 40). Just as the human body is organized, the Lord has designed specific roles for men, and unique functions for women, within the body of believers.

Prayer Points:

Based on the following verses, what is the function of men in the church?

1.   I Timothy 3:1-13

2.   I Timothy 2:12 (implied)

3.   Titus 1:5-9

As a helper for your husband, can you think of any specific way in which you can assist him in fulfilling God's role for him in the church?

You are a sister in Christ to the men in your church. Is there any specific way in which you can encourage these brothers as they fulfill the role that God has designed for them in the church?

When the revolutionary concepts of Christianity swept through the Roman Empire during the first century A.D., fresh problems arose. For the first time, women were given equal status in worshiping God. These newly discovered freedoms often resulted in chaotic worship services within the church. The book of I Timothy was written "so that you may know how one ought to conduct himself in the household of God" (I Timothy 3:15).

Some women had become so disruptive during the church services in Corinth that Paul accused them of making up their own rules (I Corinthians 14:36). There is indication that in Ephesus there were women aggressively desiring to become teachers and exercise authority over the entire congregation (I Timothy 2:12). Immediately following Paul's reminder to the Corinthians that God is not a God of confusion, he gave much needed clarification of the woman's role in the church service.

Prayer Points:

Much of the Lord's direction regarding women's ministry roles in the church revolves around teaching. **Webster's New World College Dictionary** defines "teach" this way:

1.) to show or help (a person) to learn (how) to do something (to teach a child how to swim)

2.) to give lessons to (a student, pupil, or class); guide the studies of; instruct

3.) to give lessons in (a subject) to someone; help someone to develop (a skill or trait) (teaches French, taught him self-discipline)

4.) to provide (a person) with knowledge, insight, etc. (the accident taught her to be careful)

Biblical constraints placed on women during corporate worship are designed to reflect and protect the wife's attitude of voluntary submission to her husband, and to authority in general. (You may want to review *Ancient Paths II,* Chapters Six and Seven.) Teaching, as well as many other ministry roles within the church, is addressed in the New Testament.

What do the following verses reveal about what women ARE NOT to do during formal public worship services?

4.   I Timothy 2:11-14

Do you interpret verse 12 as being a mandate for women to be totally mute during church services?

Does I Corinthians 11:5 support your above interpretation?

What, specifically, might Paul mean when he exhorts women to "be quiet"?

Can you think of any area, other than teaching, in which a woman might be tempted to exercise, or usurp, authority over a man during public worship?

Check any areas on the following page where you may be subtly undermining your husband's authority at church:

- Do you follow your husband's lead regarding which church to attend?

- Do you ask for your husband's permission before accepting jobs or ministry opportunities at church?

- Do you attempt to pressure your husband into accepting church responsibilities that you would like for him to assume?

- When speaking with others on Sunday mornings do you dominate your husband in conversations?

- Do you sit with your husband and attend the Sunday school class of his choice?

- Do you make the decisions as to which church activities that the family will attend before consulting with your husband?

- If your husband is unsaved, do you give money to the church without his knowledge or consent?

- Do you always speak respectfully of your husband in the presence of other believers?

Optional: Look up the Greek word used for "teach" in I Timothy 2:12. Does the tense used in the word help to clarify the meaning of this text for you?

According to this verse, what should a woman NOT do during corporate worship services?

5.   I Corinthians 11:3

Draw a diagram below depicting what this verse says.

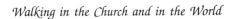

Prayer Points:

6.   I Corinthians 14:34-36

Though some see this as a command for women to not utter a word during church services, in context with verses 2-6, 9, 11, 13, 18, 19, 21, 23, 27-29 and 30, what might these verses mean?

Does self-righteous pride quietly whisper in your ear that you are more knowledgeable and spiritual than your husband? Remember that few men have as many opportunities for formal Bible study as do women with discretionary time. Take care not to "instruct" your husband on all that you have learned from the Word. Allow him to lead.

When you have a spiritual question, do you first go to your husband for the answer?   How do you think that this makes him feel?

Describe a recent experience when your husband felt that you were spiritually dependent upon him.

Should you ask your husband spiritual questions if he is unsaved? Why, or why not?

How would you demonstrate a submissive heart if your husband did not know the answer to your question?

What should single women do if they have spiritual questions?

Optional: Examples of Usurped Authority

The Old Testament stories of women usurping authority provide examples for our instruction (I Corinthians 10:11). What can you learn from the following lives?

> Eve - Genesis 3:6-19
>
> Sarai - Genesis 16:1-6; 21:1-21
>
> Rebekah - Genesis 27, 31:41
>
> Potiphar's wife - Genesis 39:7-20

Prayer Points:

What do the following verses reveal about what women ARE to do during formal public worship services?

7.   I Timothy 2:9

Do you believe that Paul is condemning braiding one's hair, having nice clothes, or wearing jewelry?

Do Proverbs 31:22 and Song of Solomon 1:9-11 support your interpretation?

The word "adorn" means "to arrange, put in order, and make ready." How do you think that this verse applies to you?

Why is a woman's appearance important in public worship?

This verse exhorts women attending church to dress with "proper clothing, modestly and discreetly." The writer's intent is to say that a woman should not dress in such a way to call attention to herself; rather, the focus of all attention should be on the Lord. When you prepare to go to church, are you careful to dress in a dignified way? (See *Ancient Paths I*, Chapter Six.)

Some clothing that women wear to church can pose an obstacle for Christian brothers who desire to focus on the Lord. When you dress for church, are you careful not to "defraud" the men in your

congregation? To "defraud" another means to "arouse desires in another that cannot be righteously satisfied." The Lord views "defrauding" your brother as being a very serious offense (I Thessalonians 4:6; Matthew 5:27, 28).

Clothing should not be selected merely on the basis of its "stylishness"; the Lord tells us not to be conformed to this world (Romans 12:2). A woman's choice of clothing should be based upon the message that she wants to convey. When you go to church, is your message more "look at me," or is it more, "look at Jesus"?

8. I Corinthians 11:3-16

On what basis does Paul appeal for women to wear head coverings during public worship?

Is this mandatory or optional? Do any verses in the text indicate that Paul leaves room for personal conviction on this issue?

How do these verses apply to you?
(Also see Romans 14:22, 23.)

The biblical mandate for women "to quietly receive instruction with entire submission" specifically relates to formal corporate worship. The wisdom of such a lifestyle is apparent since we should always be learning and growing in the knowledge of the Lord. Our attitude should always be one of humility whether we are in a church service or not.

Far from limiting women in ministry, God's Word liberates women for ministry. Throughout Scripture women are highly acclaimed and fill a vast array of ministry roles. Each woman has been created with certain specific ministries designed for her before she was even born (Ephesians 2:10).

What insights can you glean regarding women in ministry from the following verses?

9.   Acts 1:13, 14

10.   Acts 2:17, 18

11.   Acts 17:2-4

12.   Acts 17:10-12

13.   Acts 21:8, 9

14.   Acts 18:24-26

15.   Exodus 15:20

16.   Psalm 68:11

17.   Luke 1:46-55

18.   Luke 2:36-38

Prayer Points:

19.   Philippians 4:3

Prayer Points:

20.   Titus 2:3-5

When Paul commends his personal friends and co-workers in Rome, one third of those mentioned are women. It is noteworthy that he refers to the husband and wife team of Priscilla and Aquila using the same Greek word to describe them both. As equal fellow workers with the apostle, he indicates no difference or distinction between them in their ministry (Romans 16:1-16).

Women are also liberated to minister through the use of their spiritual gifts. What do these verses indicate?

21.   I Corinthians 12:1

22.   I Timothy 4:14

Are you aware of your spiritual gift?

How do you use your spiritual gift to edify other believers during formal public worship?

How do you use your spiritual gift to edify other believers outside of formal public worship?

God's Word reveals His tender love and sensitivity for women. This is evidenced by the care that He takes to encourage women who are not married. There are unique ministry opportunities for special groups of women in the church.

Two distinct groups of women are mentioned below. What insight into ministry do you note in the following verses?

23.   Luke 2:36, 37

24.   I Timothy 5:3-10, 16

Do you know any women who fall into this category? What is your responsibility toward those women?

25.   I Corinthians 7:8, 32-35

Do you know any women who fall into this category? How might you encourage them?

Few issues have been as hotly debated in the church as the biblical role of women. The subject became heated in the early church, and through the rise of twentieth century feminism it has come to a full boil in the twenty-first century.

Many biblical directives for women in the church are quite specific and direct, but what about the "gray areas"? There are valid questions in application where God seems to leave some leeway for personal conviction. For example, is it biblical for a woman to share insights from the Word in an informal group if men are present? Is it biblical for a woman to be a guest speaker during a formal worship service? Many such issues can be argued both ways.

Each believer has a responsibility to seek God's will and to be obedient. In areas that seem to be left open for personal application, there is one rule that cannot be ignored. Apply the "law of love." While legitimately claiming biblical freedom to do certain things, those actions may cause another believer to stumble spiritually.

What insights can you glean from the following verses?

26.   I Corinthians 8:9-13

If possible, describe an area in the church where women may have the liberty to do something, but where their love for others may temper their actions.

Prayer Points:

We are not to be "men pleasers," trying to align ourselves to others' legalistic personal preferences. Yet, we are to take great care that our actions do not encourage another believer to do something that she thinks is questionable. We must also protect our reputation with others so that the Lord can use us in their lives.

The limit of our liberty is the law of love. In "gray areas" we must take care not to judge others, and not to claim our own right to do things our own way. Wisdom often necessitates leaning toward the side of conservatism, taking care not to offend, or sear the conscience, of a weaker believer. We must never "do our own thing," disregarding its effect upon others.

The Lord clearly instructs women on certain issues in His Word. The directives are "black and white." Yet, many women argue with the most blatant of commands.

Why would women contest the biblical exhortation to learn quietly with a submissive attitude during public worship? Personal pride is always an obstacle to obedience. Another great hindrance is fear.

Women may be fearful that if they are quietly submissive in public worship that their ministry opportunities will be stifled, or that they will not be given the public acclaim which they feel is their due. Others may be afraid that they will never experience the depth of fulfillment and joy for which God designed them.

God, Himself, realizes that fear tends to threaten quiet submission. He encourages us by saying that women can be righteously submissive like Sarah if they "do what is right without being frightened by any fear" (I Peter 3:6).

Only when women are faithful to obey the Lord's commands can they experience the depth of blessing and ministry that He has intended for their lives.

"If you keep My commandments- if you continue to obey My instructions - you will abide in My love and live on in it; ... I have told you these things that My joy and delight may be in you, and that your joy and gladness may be full measure and complete and overflowing."
(John 15:10a, 11; Amplified New Testament)

Prayer Points:

The Lord's command for women to quietly receive instruction with entire submissiveness is directed toward both actions and attitudes.

➤ In light of today's lesson, is there anything that you are actively doing in your public worship life that needs to be changed? If so, what steps do you need to take?

➤ In the area of public worship, do you have any attitudes that need to change? If so, what steps do you need to take?

➤ Is it your commitment to obey the Lord? If so, tell Him now. Then, begin this moment to implement any necessary changes that His Spirit has revealed to you through the Word.

Prayer Points:

SUMMARY:

Define "quietly receiving instruction with entire submissiveness" in your own terms. You could use a synonym, a motto, a poem or a prayer, or even make a drawing to show your understanding of this concept.

DISCUSSION:

Ask an older sister in Christ if she has noticed any change in the roles of women in the church over the years. If change has been noted, what factors might have contributed to that change?

APPLICATION:

Your college-aged son attends a Christian group at his university. A woman leader instructs the group on Christian doctrine and living. Your son asks you if this is biblical. What is your response?

CHAPTER FIVE

OLDER WOMEN TEACH AND ENCOURAGE THE YOUNG WOMEN

Eagerly embracing my God-given ministry role as a woman in the church.

"Older women likewise are to be ... teaching what is good, that they may encourage the young women..."
Titus 2:3, 4

"She opens her mouth in wisdom, and the teaching of kindness is on her tongue."
Proverbs 31:26

Prayer Points:

"Older women likewise are to be ... teaching what is good, that they may encourage the young women..."
Titus 2:3, 4

"She opens her mouth in wisdom, and the teaching of kindness is on her tongue."
Proverbs 31:26

"There is no substitute for a good teacher." While the Lord has excluded women from formally teaching men, He has said in His Word that godly older women are the best teachers for young women in the church. Older women have acquired credentials unmatched by any other group.

Godly older women have a track record. Only another woman can begin to understand the ups and downs of life that other women face. Older women have "walked a mile in your shoes"; perhaps they have walked several miles in those shoes. They know what those shoes feel like, they've experienced the same blisters, and they even know what it is like to have holes worn in their soles.

The honor and responsibility of teaching both children and younger women is a high calling. While men and women alike are responsible to teach their children (Proverbs 6:20; 31:1; II Timothy 1:5; 3:15), only godly older women are specifically mandated to teach the younger women.

By the time a woman has successfully raised her children, she has garnered a wealth of experience and information. Rather than sensing a loss of purpose in life when children leave home, women are assigned a specific purpose from God. Perhaps if more older women took seriously the Lord's call to teach young women, there would be fewer victims of the "empty nest syndrome" which stymies so many.

The contemporary church, and society in general, is feeling the effects of the failure of women today to fulfill their God-appointed tasks.

1.   Hosea 4:1-3, 6

        What results from a lack of knowledge of God?

What evidences of this do you see in society today?

Some women may argue that teaching is reserved for the select few upon which the spiritual gift of teaching is bestowed. While teaching is a specific spiritual gift given to some women in the church (Romans 12:6, 7; I Corinthians 12:28, 29), we see in Scripture that all women are to be teaching.

God has appointed certain tasks for each individual to fulfill. We have the option of either voluntarily and cheerfully cooperating with Him or not. There is a reward for obedience (I Corinthians 9:16, 17).

Each woman is teaching something through the life that she lives and through the words that she speaks. The question is, are we teaching what God would have us to teach, in the way that He would have us to teach it?

1. We Teach Through Our Example

Someone once said, "Your actions speak so loudly that I can't hear what you're saying." The example set in one's daily living can either establish or deny a forum for verbal instruction. Like it or not, others are watching.

What do the following texts reveal about teaching through example?

2. Philippians 3:17; 4:9

   Would you recommend that your children speak the way that they have heard you speak in your home?

   Are you a visible model of godliness as others see you waiting in long checkout lines in grocery stores?

3. I Corinthians 4:16; 11:1

4. I Thessalonians 1:6

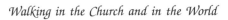

Prayer Points:

5.   II Thessalonians 3:7-9

Can you unhesitatingly exhort others to follow the example that you set in your life?

Are there any specific areas which you would hesitate to exhibit as an example for others?

How could you better please the Lord in this area?

6.   I Peter 3:1, 2

How might an unsaved husband be won to the Lord?

Our family watches our lives. How we live affects our husband and children with eternal consequences. Though we may be unaware of it, we are teaching others through our example.

A picture is worth a thousand words and what others see in our lives speaks volumes. Our lives are a "sermon in shoes" with every step taken becoming a dissertation on the divine. Others are observing and noting if we are truly "walking the walk" and not merely "talking the talk."

Our example does matter.

II.   We Teach Through Our Words

While the Lord calls some women to teach through formal Bible study formats, most teaching done by women is on an informal basis. Each time that we speak with another there is an opportunity to teach and encourage.

The Lord has specified seven "good things" that older women are to teach young women.

7.   Titus 2:4, 5

List the seven "good things" that older women are to teach and encourage the younger women to do.

a)

b)

c)

d)

e)

f)

g)

In which of these seven areas do you feel most qualified to teach another woman?

In which areas do you feel a need for further instruction in your own life?

Complete the following table. Give ideas for how you might personally encourage a young woman in specific areas of her life. Consider what advice you have received in the past that has particularly exhorted you. If you have received bits of advice from older women, which did not convey encouragement, note that also. Record these pitfalls which you should attempt to avoid as you discuss life issues with another woman.

Prayer Points:

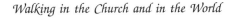

Titus Teaching Tips

Prayer Points:

Teach "Good Things"	Practical Ideas for Encouraging	Pitfalls to Avoid (things not to say)
Love Their Husbands		
Love Their Children		
Be Sensible		
Be Pure		
Be Workers at Home		
Be Kind		
Be Subject to Their Own Husbands		

Discerning older women often encounter Christian women trapped in sinful attitudes or actions who desperately need teaching and encouragement. Occasionally, these weaker sisters resist sound teaching and refuse to be encouraged.

In situations where a problem needs to be addressed, the mature believer is to respectfully appeal to older women as mothers and to younger women as sisters (I Timothy 5:1, 2).

What insights can you glean from the following verses regarding instructing a sinning sister?

Prayer Points:

8.   Titus 1:13

9.   Titus 2:15

10.   II Timothy 2:24-26

11.   II Timothy 4:2

12.   II Thessalonians 3:14, 15

13.   Ephesians 5:11

14.   II Corinthians 2:6-8

More often than not, believing women are hungering and thirsting for direction and encouragement. Rather than resenting God's truth, they delight to know that another woman is standing with them in life.

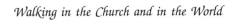

Paul exhorts us to "encourage one another, and build up one another" (I Thessalonians 5:11).

Prayer Points:

> **Optional:* What does it mean to "encourage" another believer? Using your concordance and expository dictionary, describe the nuances of the term as used in Acts 18:27 and John 11:19, 31.

What do you learn about encouraging others from the following texts?

15. Acts 11:23, 24

16. Romans 1:12

17. Hebrews 3:13

18. Hebrews 10:25

In order to encourage and instruct our sisters in Christ most effectively, we must know God's Word. What do the following verses reveal regarding specific ways to encourage others using Scripture?

19. I Thessalonians 4:18 and 5:11

    According to the preceding verses, what "words" will comfort (encourage) others?

20.   Colossians 3:16

Would others say that the word of Christ richly dwells in you?

Do you speak to others in this manner?

What steps might you take to improve in this area?

It is God's desire that older women teach and encourage young women in His church. In prior generations it was common for women to congregate regularly during general daily activities. When Jesus walked the earth women habitually met at the water well in town (John 4:6, 7). What other natural opportunities for meeting, teaching and encouraging were common during biblical times?

21.   Acts 2:42, 46

22.   Luke 2:36-38

23.   Luke 1:39-56

You have comparable opportunities in your own life. In our fast-paced, regimented world, it is becoming increasingly difficult to meet with other women. Yet, opportunities still exist. List the different lifestyle opportunities that you have when you might teach other women, or to be instructed by other women.

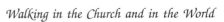

Prayer Points:

Whenever we are with other people, we are representatives of God Almighty (II Corinthians 5:20). Each time that you encounter another person, ask the Lord if He has a message that He would like to give to them through you. How thrilling it is to live with the understanding that every encounter with others is a "divine appointment!"

Mothers, mother-in-laws, and grandmothers, provide a great resource for teaching. The church desperately needs older women to disciple those who are younger. Since most young women do not live in close proximity to their extended families, they are desperate for someone to show them the "ancient paths" for successful living.

If you are a young woman, ask the Lord to place you under the tutorship of an older woman who exemplifies reverent behavior. Then commit to nurturing a teachable heart. Older women may be intimidated by a young woman who seems to know everything. You may even need to take the initiative, prayerfully approaching an older woman to request her input.

If you are an older woman, covenant with God to be faithful in this area of teaching and encouraging other Christian women. Don't miss opportunities for obedience by claiming personal inadequacy (Exodus 4:12). Instead, believe the Lord when He promises, "I will be with your mouth, and teach you what you are to say" (Exodus 4:12). Ask the Lord to give you eyes to see the needs of those around you, and ask Him to give you boldness as you encourage and teach "good things" to other women (Ephesians 6:19, 20).

SUMMARY:

Define what it means for "older women to teach and encourage young women" in your own terms. You could uses a synonym, a motto, a poem or a prayer, or even make a drawing to show your understanding of this concept.

Prayer Points:

DISCUSSION:

According to Titus 2:3, what would make an older woman qualified to teach and encourage a young woman?

How might an older woman encourage and teach a younger single woman?

APPLICATION:

An older woman has committed herself to developing a teaching and encouraging relationship with a young mom in your church. The older woman feels awkward and intimidated by formal "teaching" situations, and asks you for suggestions on how to go about befriending this young mom. What advice do you give?

UNIT TWO

WALKING IN THE WORLD

**"Therefore be careful how you walk, not as unwise men,
but as wise, making the most of your time, because the days are evil."
Ephesians 5:15, 16**

Unit Chapters:

6.   Be Pure - Titus 2:5

7.   Do Not Dishonor the Word of God -
Titus 2:5; I Timothy 5:14

CHAPTER SIX

BE PURE

*Becoming more like Jesus
and refusing to compromise with the world.*

**"Encourage the young women to be... pure..."
Titus 2:4, 5**

"Encourage the young women to be ... pure..."
Titus 2:4, 5

Prayer Points:

The environmentally conscious of our day decry the perils of polluted air, contaminated waters, toxic soils, and chemically tainted foods. Such physical threats have sounded a global alarm for environmental purity.

The world is also a dangerous place spiritually. God, through His Word, has sounded a global alarm to His people for spiritual purity.

As a Christian living on earth, do you ever feel like a round peg in a square hole? Do you feel like you just don't fit? Do you seem to be marching to the beat of a different Drummer? If so, be encouraged. You are not alone. What do you see in the following verses about believers living on earth?

1.   Philippians 3:20, 21

2.   Ephesians 2:19

3.   Hebrews 11:13

4.   I Peter 1:1

5.   I Peter 2:11

As "aliens" on earth, we sense that we "don't belong"; as "strangers" on the planet, we simply "don't fit." This is our temporary home.

Life on earth is a combat zone as war is being waged on our souls. Scripture tells us that when we lose skirmishes in this war, the ensuing sin makes "a separation between you and your God" (Isaiah 59:2).

Since God knows that we don't belong here, and that we are subject to painfully destructive sin, why does He intentionally leave us in such a dangerous place? Why aren't we immediately taken to be with Him the moment that we become saved?

6.　　John 17:14-20

Who is praying this prayer on behalf of believers?

Is He aware of the danger to which believers are exposed?

What does He specifically pray?

How are believers sanctified (purified, made holy)?

Why are believers left on earth?

Do you see any specific reference to yourself here? (☺!)

Satan is temporarily the god of this world (II Corinthians 4:4) and he rules with evil intent (John 8:44; 12:31). Earth is, indeed, a hostile environment for believers. Yet, the Lord knowingly sent us into this environment.

Looking down the corridors of time, Christ saw each of us and prayed for us. As one of His final acts in life, He prayed that we would be sanctified, made holy and pure.

Throughout Scripture, we are exhorted to be pure (I Timothy 5:22; Titus 2:4, 5; I Peter 1:16; 3:2). The term "pure" is translated "chaste" in many Bible translations. Why does the Lord desire that we be pure?

7.   Matthew 5:8

Prayer Points:

What does it mean to be pure? **Webster's New World College Dictionary** defines "pure" this way:

1.) free from anything that adulterates; unmixed (pure maple syrup)..
2.) free from anything that taints, impairs, infects; clear (pure water or air)
3.) simpler; mere (pure luck)
4.) utter; absolute; sheer (pure lunacy)
5.) free from defects; perfect; faultless; free from sin or guilt; blameless
6.) virgin or chaste
7.) of unmixed stock; pure-bred
8.) in the Bible, ceremonially undefiled

In Scripture, the Greek word, "hagnos," means chaste, clean, modest, perfect, pure, immaculate, clear, holy, and free from admixture of evil.

When comparing ourselves with others, we might conclude that we are doing well on the "purity scale." Yet, what is our standard for purity?

8.   Psalm 12:6; 19:8; 119:40

9.   Isaiah 6:3

10.   Hebrews 7:26

11.   I John 3:3

We are called to be pure, and the Lord is our example. Jesus did not cloister Himself away in order to protect Himself from being defiled. As He daily rubbed shoulders with the filth of human sin, He Himself remained pure.

Like Christ, we are called to go into the world. Jesus prayed that Christians would boldly venture from their church buildings and lead the unsaved to salvation (John 17). We are to be "IN the world, but not OF the world." As D. L. Moody said, "The ship belongs in the water of the world, but if the water gets in the ship, it sinks." We are to mingle in the world without merging with it. We are to be pure.

Prayer Points:

How can women of God remain pure in an evil world? How can we keep from getting "mixed up" in the world? Scripture provides several answers to that question.

I.   Be Separated from Evil

What insights can you glean from the following texts?

12.   Psalm 101:6, 7

13.   Ephesians 5:8-13

14.   I Peter 4:3-5

15.   Revelation 18:4, 5

16.   II Corinthians 6:14 - 7:1

> To what types of relationships might this apply?

> Are you involved in any relationship that does not honor the Lord?

Has another person's behavior begun to control or negatively influence your behavior, time, resources, etc?

Prayer Points:

Does another person's resistance to your attempt to pull him/her along limit or control your behavior? (Imagine yourself yoked in the harness with another person. As you pull forward, if the other person is not pulling in the same direction, or exerting the same amount of strength as you are, the result will be that you will wind up "going in circles.")

What should you do about this situation?

Optional: Using your concordance and Greek dictionary, look up the meanings of the words "unequally yoked together." What do you learn that might give insight into the nature of the relationship being discussed?

17. Deuteronomy 7:3, 4
    What are you to do if you are already married to an unbeliever? (See I Peter 3:1, 2; I Corinthians 7:13-16)

II. Do Not Love the World

18. I John 2:15, 16

List, in the order given, the three elements that constitute "all that is in the world."

a. _____ ("desiring to satisfy sensual,
                                physical cravings")

b. _____ ("seeing and wanting to possess")

c. _____ ("pride in status, money,
                                education, appearance,
                                reputation, etc.")

**Prayer
Points:**

Give an example of each of these elements as you have observed
them operating in your own life.

    a.

    b.

    c.

19.   Romans 12:2

The word "conformed" means "to be squeezed into a mold." Is there
any area of your life where you sense that the world may be putting
the squeeze on you?

    What should you do about this situation?

20.   Mark 4:18, 19

21.   Matthew 16:25

The biblical story of Lot provides us with an example of one who loved
the world, and subsequently mixed with the world.

22.   Genesis 13:9-13

    On what basis did Lot make his decision?

Do you see any evidence of Lot loving the world?

**Prayer
Points:**

Would you have approached making this decision differently if you had been Lot? If so, how?

There is a progression of conformity to a sinful world. It has been said that "every compromise involves two surrenders." The pathway of small compromises is a slippery slope. When sin is accommodated, more sin follows. What progression do you see in the following verses?

23.   Genesis 13:12; 14:12; 19:1

24.   Genesis 19:1-26

What was the result of Lot succumbing to loving the world?

Why do think that Lot's wife looked back?

Is there anything (or anyone) in your life on which you would have trouble turning your back?

"Everything created by God is good." The world itself, though temporarily Satan's domain, is not evil. The proper response to things of the world is that "it is received with gratitude," and our loving Creator is given glory (I Timothy 4:4). Sin enters into the picture when we begin to love the world rather than the Lord. God tells us that every created thing "is sanctified by the means of the word of God and prayer" (I Timothy 4:5).

III. Be Separated From Blatantly Sinning Believers

Purity can be undermined by false teaching in the church, and also by habitual sin being allowed to persist within the Body of Christ.

Jesus warned the disciples to "watch out and beware the leaven of the Pharisees and Sadducees" (Matthew 16:6-12). False teaching gone unchallenged can permeate and defile an entire church. The Lord likens it to leaven.

Leaven is a substance that has a silent, pervasive influence. When left unhindered, it promotes fermentation. Paul tells the churches to clean out the old leaven since "a little leaven leavens the whole lump of dough" (I Corinthians 5:6, 7; Galatians 5:9).

Like false teaching, when sin is allowed to go unchecked it is like leaven in the church. It taints everything it touches.

What insights can you glean from the following text?

25.   I Corinthians 5:7-13

What should be our response to a worldly non-Christian who sins?

What should be our response to an unrepentant Christian who persists in sin?

Have you ever had an experience where another believer's sin encouraged you to make personal compromises?

Sin in the ranks is a very serious thing. After first "judging ourselves" (I Corinthians 11:28; II Corinthians 13:5), believers should seek to prayerfully discern and properly evaluate sin among the body of believers. Christ wants us to be discerning and able to judge (Matthew 7:16-20; Philippians 1:9, 10).

Prayer Points:

Yet, "judging others" is always to be done with the heartfelt motive of love, never with condemnation. The goal is always to be the repentance and restoration of the one trapped in sin (II Corinthians 2:6, 7) The Lord has given believers appropriate steps to follow in addressing sin in the church (Matthew 18:15-17).

The purity of the entire church is adversely affected by the presence of one unrepentant sinner in the midst.

IV. Be Like Christ

Christians are called to be pure, as Christ Himself is pure (I John 3:3). Purity is an impossible goal to attain in our own strength. It is only through the empowering work of the Holy Spirit in our lives that we can experience victory over sin.

God Himself instills the desire to obey Him, and infuses the power to follow through on those desires. "It is God who is at work in you, both to will and to work for His good pleasure" (Philippians 2:13). We cannot become like Christ through our efforts, but we can become like Him as God works in our lives.

How does the Lord want us to live in this world?

26.   Matthew 5:13-16

        To what two things did Jesus liken the Christian life?

        How are these two things examples of purity?

Both salt and light make their presence known. Salt acts secretly and must interact to be of value. Light acts publicly and instantly dispels darkness.

Salt is well known as a flavor enhancer. It is also used in food preservation as it helps to prevent deterioration. Salt can be used to curtail the undesired growth of organisms (Judges 9:45). It also possesses great healing qualities.

Light provides brightness that exposes sin and promotes goodness (Ephesians 5:8-13). Jesus is the Light of the world (John 8:12). As we are in constant contact with the Light, we reflect Christ in our lives. Paul calls believers "luminaries" in the midst of a crooked and perverse world (Philippians 2:15).

Prayer Points:

What in the world are you doing? Is the saltiness in your life pure? Does your life make those in the world thirsty for Christ? How is your life like salt?   (get specific)

Is the light emanating from your life pure and bright? Do the good works in your life cause people who see you to glorify God? How is your life like a light?   (get specific)

The Lord blesses the pure in heart and longs to pour added blessing into our lives. Jesus said that we are made pure and sanctified through the word (John 17:17). We are to set our thoughts on things that are pure (Philippians 4:8).

27.   I Thessalonians 5:21-23

        What are you to do?

        What does God Himself do?

Paul says that his desire is to "present you as a pure virgin" to Christ (II Corinthians 11:2). While waiting for the imminent coming of our Lord Jesus Christ, make it your conviction to remain pure in an impure world.

Prayer Points:

A belief is something that you hold; a conviction is something that holds you. Do you have personal convictions that hold you back from impure living? If not, ask the Lord to sensitize your heart toward sin, and instill convictions that please Him.

As you minister in the world, refuse to get "mixed up" with it. While daily rubbing shoulders with sinners, commit to being separated from evil. Love the sinner; hate the sin.

Fight the world's attempt to squeeze you into its mold. Flee from opportunities to sin. Don't be led astray from the simplicity and purity of devotion to Christ (II Corinthians 11:3). Fall more in love with Jesus; resist the world's efforts to seduce you.

We will see Him soon. Be pure.

**"'Come out from their midst and be separate,' says the Lord.
'And do not touch what is unclean; and I will welcome you.'"
II Corinthians 6:17**

SUMMARY:

Define being "pure" in your own terms. You could use a synonym, a motto, a poem or a prayer, or even make a drawing to show your understanding of this character trait.

Prayer Points:

DISCUSSION:

When God judged Sodom and Gomorrah, Lot and his family were almost destroyed. Would it always be WRONG to live in a town like Sodom, or can you think of any situation where moving there might be the RIGHT thing to do?

APPLICATION:

Your teenage daughter has a new set of friends whose lifestyle is questionable. Though your daughter maintains that she is attempting to share Christ with these girls, you are concerned about their influence on her life. What do you do?

CHAPTER SEVEN

DO NOT DISHONOR THE WORD OF GOD

*Living in such a way
that would bring honor to the name of Christ.*

**"...encourage the young women...
that the word of God may not be dishonored."
Titus 2:5**

**"...younger widows... give the enemy no
occasion for reproach..."
I Timothy 5:14**

"encourage the young women... that the word of God may not be dishonored." Titus 2:5

Prayer Points:

"younger widows... give the enemy no occasion for reproach" Timothy 5:14

You are being watched. The movements that you make are being monitored. Your words are being weighed. Your decisions are being scrutinized. Even your attitudes are being evaluated.

As followers of the Lord Jesus, it is important that we realize that God is watching us (Psalm 139:2), angels are watching (I Corinthians 4:9; Hebrews 12:1; Daniel 4:3), other believers are watching (I Timothy 4:12), and the unbelieving world is watching our lives (II Corinthians 3:2).

Much hinges upon what these observers view in our lives. God, in His providence, has chosen to link His own reputation with ours. The Lord God Almighty has entrusted His children with an incredible responsibility in this world; He has put His own reputation on the line by the way that we live our lives!

Much as a child may bring honor or dishonor to the family name by his personal conduct, "Christ"ians may bring honor or dishonor to the name of Christ by the way that they conduct themselves. What a sobering thought.

What do the following verses reveal about God's name and reputation being at stake in the lives of His people?

1.   Psalm 23:3

2.   Psalm 25:11

3.   Psalm 31:3

4.   Isaiah 52:4, 5

5.   Ezekiel 36:22, 23

God's holy name can be blasphemed, or dishonored, by the way that His own people live. The Greek word "blasphemeo," is better translated "dishonor" in English.

Webster's New World College Dictionary defines the verb "dishonor" this way:

> *1)   to treat disrespectfully; insult.*
> *2)   to bring shame or discredit upon; disgrace*
> *3)   to violate the virginity or chastity of*
> *4)   to refuse or fail to pay (a check, draft, bill of exchange, etc.)*

Women of God are called upon to live in such a way "that the word of God may not be dishonored" (Titus 2:5). It is apparent that a Christian woman's conduct in the world can affect God's personal reputation. Any misconduct can bring disgrace and shame to the Lord.

Our enemy, Satan, maliciously looks for and capitalizes upon any sin in a Christian's life. He uses such opportunities to slander, and bring reproach on the name of Christ (I Timothy 5:14).

The world is scrutinizing the lives of believers. As we resolve to never bring dishonor on God's word, it behooves us to be aware of areas where His reputation is vulnerable. In the New Testament there seem to be two basic areas where God's reputation is especially attacked through failure in believers' lives.

The first observable area through which the world judges God's reputation is in the moral behavior of Christians. A second visible area where God's reputation may be jeopardized is in the believer's response toward authority (I Peter 2:11-15).

Prayer Points:

I. We Honor the Word of God Through Exemplary Moral Behavior

God is concerned about how His children conduct themselves in the world. Believers are exhorted to "abstain from all appearance of evil" (I Thessalonians 5:22, KJV). What do the following verses reveal about the behavior of believers toward nonbelievers?

6. I Thessalonians 4:11, 12

7. Romans 12:17-21

Any sinful or immoral behavior in the life of one who claims to follow Christ brings great dishonor to the very name of Jesus.

II. We Honor the Word of God By Respecting Authority

Non-Christians closely scrutinize the way in which God's children respond to authority in the world. What insight can you glean regarding authority systems in the world?

8. Romans 13:1-7

The failure of believers to respond correctly to authority in the home, in the workplace, and in government brings disrepute upon the name of the Lord.

9. Complete the table on the following page. Note how the Christian's moral behavior in the world, and/or response toward authority in the world, affect God's reputation in the world.

Bible Reference	**Believer's Behavior in the World**	**Believer's Attitude Toward Authority**	**Effect Upon God's Word and Reputation**
II Samuel 12:13, 14	David Sinned with Bathsheba: killed Uriah		Gave occasion for enemies of the Lord to blaspheme.
Matthew 17:24-27			
Romans 2:23, 24			
Philippians 2:14, 15			
I Timothy 2:1-4			
I Timothy 5:14			
I Timothy 6:1			
Titus 2:4, 5			
Titus 2:7, 8			
Titus 2:9, 10			
I Peter 2:11, 12			
I Peter 2:13-15			

Prayer Points:

All authority is established by God, and all authority in heaven and earth belongs to Jesus (John 19:10, 11; Matthew 28:18). Rulers are servants of God who are appointed to reward good and punish evil (I Peter 2:13, 14). Godly government is designed to provide a forum from which to live a godly and dignified life (I Timothy 2:2, 3). Christians should "seek the welfare of the city" in which they live, and "pray to the Lord on its behalf" (Jeremiah 29:7).

Christian women desire to be subject to the world's authority systems since rebellion would dishonor the Lord's reputation. God Himself says that "rebellion is as the sin of witchcraft" (I Samuel 15:23). Yet, as the darkness of the last days intensifies, one must ask if there is ever a biblically justifiable case for civil disobedience.

What insights can you glean from the following passages regarding godly civil disobedience?

10.   Daniel 3

11.   Daniel 6

12.   Acts 4:18-20

13.   Acts 5:27-29, 40-42

Civil disobedience is a very serious matter since God's reputation is at stake. Any decision to disobey established law must involve a thorough understanding of God's Word, time spent prayerfully seeking the Lord's will, and the input of wise counsel.

Disobedience should be considered only as a last resort after making an appeal to the appropriate authorities, and exhausting all legal options (Acts 28:18, 19). (For specific instruction regarding steps involved in making an appeal, see "How to Make an Appeal" at the end of this chapter.) Should disobedience become necessary, one should be prepared to graciously accept the consequences (I Peter 3:13-15; Esther 4:16).

Married Christian women are to be subject to their own husband's leadership in any decision regarding civil disobedience. Take care not to disobey God by usurping your husband's authority in a pious attempt to protest ungodly governmental authority.

God instructs us to pray for those in authority. Remember, He can change people and circumstances when we cannot (Daniel 4:28-37; Proverbs 21:1).

Why is God concerned that His reputation with worldly unbelievers is held high? The Creator of all life is not insecurely looking for affirmation from human sinners. Neither is He arrogantly demanding their adulation because it is His due.

The Lord God loves sinners. The penalty for sin is death. God gave His only Son, Jesus, to die for each person on earth. The Father wants His reputation established so that individuals will hear that He loves them, and that through Christ they may have eternal life (I Corinthians 10:32, 33). He "desires all men to be saved and to come to the knowledge of the truth" (I Timothy 2:4).

This "good news" of salvation through Christ is called the gospel.

What do the following verses reveal about how we can honor God's Word and reputation?

14.	Matthew 28:18-20

15.	Luke 24:46, 47

16.	Acts 1:8

List the places where you "rub shoulders with the world" on a regular basis; such as home, neighborhood, schools, stores, jobs, sports, clubs, etc.:

What does the Lord want you to do in those places?

Prayer Points:

17. Acts 8:35

How was Philip prepared for this encounter?

Are you prepared if the Lord gives you such an opportunity?

18. Colossians 4:2-6

Do you feel that you are able to make the message of Christ clear to others?

Briefly describe a recent personal encounter when you had the opportunity to tell a non-Christian about Christ.

What could you have done differently to have made the most of that opportunity?

What insights about witnessing do you glean from these Colossian verses?

19. I Peter 3:15, 16

What are believers to do?

When are they to do it?

With what attitude are they to do it?

To be a witness means to "attest of a fact, or give a firsthand account of something." As children of God, we are the only people on earth who can give a firsthand, personal account of Christ's provision of salvation.

To give a testimony means to give "a declaration or statement made to establish a fact; any form of evidence." Any time that believers exhibit evidence of Christ in their lives, they are giving a testimony to the world. If you were accused of being a Christian, would there enough evidence in your life to get you convicted?

20.   Ephesians 6:19, 20

        How does Paul say that believers ought to speak?

        Would you say that your testimony for Christ is bold, or are you more of a "secret service," "undercover" Christian?

Many believers are hesitant to be outspoken about Jesus Christ because they fear personal rejection. Satan tries to bully believers into thinking that the world is not interested in hearing the life-giving, good news of the gospel. Yet, what does God say?

21.   Ezekiel 2:4-7

22.   I Peter 3:14

23.   Isaiah 52:7

God, in His wisdom has placed the church in charge of spreading the gospel on earth. We are the church. YOU are the dwelling place of God's Holy Spirit. How are you doing with the assignment that God has given you to be His witness?

Prayer Points:

Do you know how to share your personal testimony with others?

Prayer Points:

> **Optional:* Read Acts 22:1-21. Paul's personal testimony is divided into three parts:
>
> - **a)** *his life before he knew Christ (verses 1-5);*
> - **b)** *his encounter with Christ (verses 6-10);*
> - **c)** *his life after meeting Christ (verses 11-21).*
>
> Using this basic outline, prepare your own story of what Christ has done in your life. Begin by jotting down notes in the appropriate column. Later, weave these events into a cohesive story. It would be beneficial to verbally share this story with another believer.
>
> [Note: If you became a believer when you were young, you might focus more on what He has done in your life as you have matured in Him.]
>
> Be sure to include information on "how to be saved" so that others will understand how to receive Christ personally.
>
> | | |
> |---|---|
> | *My Life Before Receiving Christ* | |
> | *How I Received Christ* | |
> | *My Life Since I Received Christ* | |

The unbelieving world is carefully watching. The ways that Christian women behave morally, and their attitudes toward authority, give the world an opinion of the Savior. God's reputation is at stake in **YOU**. God's purpose is that men and women will come to know His saving grace through Christ. Our lives may either repel or attract unbelievers to the Lord. We carry an awesome responsibility.

As women of the Word walking in the world, great care must be taken to live above reproach. In light of today's lesson, is there any area of moral behavior in your life that needs to be changed in order to not dishonor our Lord?

Prayer Points:

In light of today's lesson, do you have any wrong attitudes toward authority which need to change in order not to dishonor our Lord?

God is honored and glorified when unbelievers come to know His Son. We must testify of Christ by the way that we live, and we must also be prepared to verbally bear witness of Christ to unbelievers.

The days are evil. Time is growing short. Daily we interact with those who are on the road to an eternity in hell. We talk of weather, wallpaper, and window-shopping. Yet, we politely evade the real issue of life; Jesus Christ died for sinners.

Though the world may see that we are different, they may never really know why. We claim that we don't want to "preach" at them. We don't want them to feel "uncomfortable." So we exist in cordial comfort, watching them walk into eternal hell.

Soon, the trumpet will sound and we will be gone (I Thessalonians 4:16, 17). As you rise into the clouds to meet the Lord, whose face will you see left behind as you take one last glance over your shoulder?

What will you do today?

"Therefore be careful how you walk, not as unwise men, but as wise, making the most of your time, because the days are evil."
Ephesians 5:15, 16

HOW TO MAKE AN APPEAL

In the first chapter of Daniel we find a handsome Jewish teenager who had been taken captive to Babylon (1:1-3). His intelligence, understanding, discerning knowledge and general ability made Daniel stand out in the crowd (1:4), and he was selected to be trained for the king's personal service (1:5).

As part of his training, Daniel was ordered to eat the king's choice food and to drink wine (1:5). This presented a dilemma for Daniel since it violated his personal spiritual convictions (1:8). It behooves us to note the steps that Daniel took in order to make an appropriate appeal.

1.   *Discern the heart motive of the one in authority:*
Daniel understood that the motive of his superiors was to improve his health and his appearance before the king (1:10).

2.   *Acknowledge and respect their motives:*
Daniel did not argue with the goals of his leaders. He found common ground, and agreed that these goals were worthy (1:12, 13).

3.   *Ask permission to suggest a creative alternative:*
Daniel respectfully requested that he be permitted to attain the king's goals using a method which offered a "win-win" solution for both parties (1:8, 12, 13).

4.   *Graciously accept the decision of the authority as God's will:*
Daniel asked for permission to try the "Jewish diet" for ten days. The results were superior, and Daniel's commitment to maintain his spiritual conviction was authorized (1:11-16).

While we must realize that all authority is established by God (Romans 13:1), and we are to thank God for everything in our lives because it is God's will for us (I Thessalonians 5:16-18), what should be our response if those in authority command us to disobey God's law?

5.   *Graciously accept the consequence if you must disobey:*
Daniel was not forced to disobey God at this time in his life. Yet, he had "made up his mind" that he would not disobey God's law, regardless of the king's decree (1:8).

Later in Daniel's life, we see that he quietly refused to obey the king's order to stop praying to God (6:1-17). He did not argue or defend himself when he was thrown into the lions den. Daniel trusted God, and he was supernaturally protected (6:16-24).

If we must disobey human authority on biblical grounds, we must be willing to graciously suffer the consequences for the glory of God. The Lord is in control of those in authority over us (Proverbs 21:1), and He is in control of every detail of our lives. We can trust Him!

Prayer Points:

SUMMARY:

Define "not dishonoring the word of God" in your own terms. You could use a synonym, a motto, a poem or a prayer, or even make a drawing to show your understanding of this concept.

DISCUSSION:

Many Christians believe that verbal "witnessing" is to be done only by those who have been given the spiritual gift of evangelism. What do you think of this?

APPLICATION:

A godly Christian woman in your community has taken a strong biblical stand against abortion. As an active clinic protester she is willing to go to jail for her convictions. Her husband has asked that she curtail her involvement so that she will not be arrested. What should she do?

UNIT THREE

KEEP WALKING!

"Finally then, brethren, we request and exhort you in the Lord Jesus, that, as you received from us instruction as to how you ought to walk and please God (just as you actually do walk), that you may excel still more."
I Thessalonians 4:1

Unit Chapter:

8. Be Faithful In All Things - I Timothy 3:11

CHAPTER EIGHT

BE FAITHFUL IN
ALL THINGS

*Relying on the Holy Spirit to enable me
to trust and obey Jesus in every area of my life.*

"Women must likewise be... faithful in all things."
I Timothy 3:11

"Women must likewise be... faithful in all things."
I Timothy 3:11

Prayer Points:

The Lord is looking for faithful women. He seeks women who are committed to knowing Him, constant in obedience, and resolute in their walk with Him. He is looking for women who faithfully keep walking on the "ancient paths."

"For the eyes of the Lord move to and fro throughout the earth that He may strongly support those whose heart is completely His" (II Chronicles 16:9).

The Lord is keenly aware of our walk with Him. He observes our faithfulness as we walk in our homes, in our churches, and in the world.

It delights the Lord to see faithful women. Without faith it is impossible to please God (Hebrews 11:6). He makes the lives of faithful women fruitful, and He uses them in ways that He does not use others (I Corinthians 4:2).

The Christian's calling is high (Philippians 3:14), and it is holy (II Timothy 1:9). God calls us to walk in a manner worthy of that calling (Ephesians 4:1). He calls women to be faithful.

Webster's New World College Dictionary defines "faithful" this way:

> 1) *keeping faith; maintaining allegiance; constant; loyal (faithful friends)*
> 2) *marked by or showing a strong sense of duty or responsibility; conscientious (faithful attendance)*
> 3) *accurate; reliable; exact (a faithful copy)*
> 4) *(Obs.) full of faith, esp. religious faith – the faithful.*
>   *a) the true believers (in any specified religion)*
>   *b) the loyal adherents or supporters*
>
> *SYN. – faithfulness implies steadfast adherence to a person or thing to which one is bound as by an oath or obligation (a faithful wife)*

Faithfulness is a divine quality. God the Father is faithful (I Thessalonians 5:24). Christ's very name is Faithful (Revelation 19:11), and faithfulness is the fruit of the Holy Spirit (Galatians 5:22).

Zealous young Christians begin their walk with the Lord with sincere intentions to always walk faithfully. God tells us that "a faithful man abounds in blessings" (Proverbs 28:20).

The Lord is looking for women to bless. He seeks women who are "faithful in all things" (I Timothy 3:11), women who are totally His in every area of their lives.

Sadly, many can become sidetracked or derailed while walking the "ancient paths" and faithfulness can become a rare commodity. The Lord says, "Many a man proclaims his own loyalty, but who can find a trustworthy man?" (Proverbs 20:6).

What happens along life's path to discourage women of God from walking with Him? Why would a Christian woman change course in life and lose her desire to be faithful?

Prayer Points:

In order to continue walking faithfully we must never lose sight of these things:

> **A. Purpose - Don't lose sight of who you are.**
>
> **B. Power - Don't lose sight of Who God is.**
>
> **C. Perspective - Don't lose sight of where you're headed.**
>
> **D. Prize and Praise - Don't lose sight of what awaits you.**

Each of these elements of walking faithfully are examined below:

A. PURPOSE: Don't lose sight of who you are.

Why are you on earth? What is your purpose in life? It is imperative that Christian women grapple with these questions. In order to know how to invest time and energies, it is necessary to have a sense of life-call and purpose.

In order to be faithful, one must have a sense of expectations and purpose. God, the Father, has a special plan for each of His children. What do the following verses reveal about your purpose in life?

Prayer Points:

1. Jeremiah 29:11

2. Acts 13:36

3. Romans 8:28, 29

4. I Corinthians 6:20

5. I Corinthians 10:31

6. Ephesians 2:10

7. Ephesians 5:8, 10, 17

8. Philippians 3:8-10

9. Colossians 1:10

10. II Thessalonians 1:11, 12

11. Titus 2:14

Describe what you perceive to be your own purpose in life:

The Lord values and ascribes great individual dignity to each of our lives. We can be assured that He has a high call and a holy plan uniquely for us. Such confidence inspires great enthusiasm as one begins walking with the Lord.

Committed to faithfulness, zealous believers who launch out ready to "conquer the world" may find themselves suffering from battle fatigue somewhere down the road. These waylaid warriors who began with a keen sense of purpose, often discover that they have lost their power to persevere.

B. POWER: Don't lose sight of Who God is.

Well-intentioned Christians, desirous of living a faithful life, can lose stride in their walk with God when they take their eyes off of Him. Much as Peter's ability to walk on water was dependent upon keeping his eyes on Jesus [Matthew 14:28-30], our walk with the Lord is dependent upon keeping our eyes on Him.

We must focus on the face of our sovereign God Who rules every detail of life. He possesses all knowledge, ability, and power. He is holy and just. He loves us. "He is a rewarder of those who seek Him" (Hebrews 11:6). We must focus on Him.

Believers are by definition embroiled in warfare. What do the following Scriptures reveal about the nature of this battle?

12.   I Samuel 17:42-47

13.   Ephesians 5:15, 16

14.   Ephesians 6:10-13

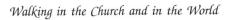

**Prayer
Points:**

Optional: Using your concordance and Greek dictionary, do a topical study on the words used to describe the "full armor of God" in Ephesians 6:13-17.

15.   I Peter 5:8-11

Our focus should be on God Almighty, not on the evil one. Remember that God is in control of Satan's activities and limits his power on earth (Job 1:12; Luke 22:31, 32). Satan is already a defeated foe (John 12:31; Revelation 20:10).

Faithfulness can flounder when believers lose sight of Who God is, and begin to focus on their circumstances, or on the enemy.

Faithfulness can also falter when believers lose sight of who God is, and focus on themselves.

The Lord calls us to walk in the same manner as Jesus walked (I John 2:6). We are to "walk worthy of God" (I Thessalonians 2:12). All self-effort to duplicate the life of Christ in ours is destined to failure and frustration. It is impossible to live the Christian life in our own strength.

What do the following Scriptures reveal about the power of living the Christian life?

16.   Isaiah 40:31

17.   Zechariah 4:6

18.   Galatians 5:16

19.   Philippians 1:6

20.   Philippians 2:13

21.   I Thessalonians 5:23, 24

Would you say that you are appropriating God's power in your life, or are you trying to live the Christian life in your own strength?

Based upon the above verses, what do you need to do differently in order to be more faithful in your walk with Christ?

Mere determination does not constitute faithfulness. Frustration is inevitable when we try to live holy lives relying on ourselves. We can get so busy with the work of the Lord, that we lose sight of the Lord of the work.

We must come to a point where we are willing to give up our plans to accomplish things for God, and allow Him to accomplish His plans through us (John 21:18, 19).

We need enthusiasm! Enthusiasm literally means "one who is possessed by a god." God Almighty must possess every part of our lives. Major Ian Thomas suggests that problems arise when we replace "enthusiasm" with "men-do-siasm." True "enthusiasm" is really "Christ-do-siasm." Depending on Christ to possess us, and live through us, is the only way that we can live faithful lives.

Faithfulness results from keeping our eyes on the Source of power in our lives as we abide in Christ (John 15:1-11).

C. PERSPECTIVE: Don't lose sight of where you're going.

There is more to life than meets the eye.

Though the world tells us that "what you see is what you get," God tells us that Christians are to have a different perspective:

"We look not at the things which are seen, but at the things which are not seen; for the things which are seen are temporal, but the things which are not seen are eternal."
II Corinthians 4:18

Everything in the world attempts to distort the eternal perspective that women of God need. It is easy to become bogged down in the mire of life's problems and concerns. The maze of daily challenges can disorient believers, causing them to lose sight of their true goals and priorities.

Our faithfulness is hindered when we lose sight of where we are headed in life. A loss of perspective can cause us to become confused and compromise our commitment to staying on course.

What do the following verses reveal about the Christian's perspective and destination?

22.   I Corinthians 2:6-9

23.   II Corinthians 5:1-5

24.   Philippians 3:12-14

25.   Colossians 3:1-4

Prayer Points:

26.   I Timothy 4:7, 8

27.   Hebrews 12:1, 2

28.   Hebrews 12:22-29

29.   I Peter 4:12, 13

30.   II Peter 3:10-13

Based upon the above verses, how would you describe your destination as a child of God?

Do you think that maintaining a proper perspective of the temporal and the eternal have any affect upon your ability to remain faithful?

Why, or why not?

God's call on the believer's life is a "heavenly call" (Hebrews 3:1). Our goal is "to be sincere and blameless until the day of Christ" (Philippians 1:10). Our destiny is to be glorified with Him in heaven (Romans 8:30).

Time on earth is short. Even a long life is transitory. God compares it to withering grass and fading flowers (Isaiah 40:6-8). We all stand on the edge of eternity. What we do here determines how we will spend that eternity.

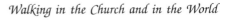

**Prayer
Points:**

When the road gets long, and weariness tempts the Christian, keeping the goal in view provides the impetus to keep going. Maintaining the proper perspective of the true destination does much to enable believers to faithfully "press on."

D. PRIZE and PRAISE: Don't lose sight of what awaits you.

All believers in Jesus Christ are going to spend eternity with Him in heaven. For every Christian to be absent from the body is to be present with the Lord (II Corinthians 5:6-8).

While the "track record" of any Christian's walk with the Lord will not disqualify him from admittance, Christians will still be judged. The judgment seat of Christ is one of reward rather than of condemnation.

Those who are "faithful in all things" will be rewarded by the Lord Jesus. Just as human parents use rewards to motivate their children, our Father's promises of rewards motivate His children.

What do the following verses reveal about the judgments and rewards of the Lord?

31.   Ecclesiastes 12:14

32.   Romans 2:16

33.   I Corinthians 3:7-15

34.   I Corinthians 4:3-5

35.   II Corinthians 5:10

Prayer Points:

36.   II Corinthians 10:18

37.   Galatians 6:7-9

38.   Colossians 3:23, 24

39.   II Timothy 4:7, 8

40.   Hebrews 11:22-26

Are you motivated to faithfulness through the promise of reward from Christ?

Why, or why not?

> *Optional:* The rewards of the Lord are often spoken of as crowns. What do you learn about crowns from I Corinthians 9:25-27; I Thessalonians 2:19; II Timothy 4:8; James 1:12; I Peter 5:4; Revelation 2:10; 3:11; 4:4, 10?

There are rewards for walking faithfully with the Lord. They will be indescribably awesome. Rather than bringing glory to one receiving the reward, these rewards will enable the child of God to truly bring more glory to the Lord (Revelation 4:10, 11). How wonderful that will be! We should all desire such an opportunity.

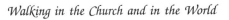

Prayer Points:

Receiving the prize is a motivation for faithful living. Yet, a greater motivation for the believer is in receiving praise from the Lord God Almighty. True faith seeks the face of God, not just the hand of God. The greatest reward will be in seeing His smile of approval.

Walking the "ancient paths" with the Lord is a lifelong journey that leads us into the arms of Jesus. As we keep our eyes on Jesus (Hebrews 12:2), and our hearts on heaven (Psalm 84:5), our pace accelerates.

Once we get a glimpse of what is awaiting us with the Lord, what was once a saunter turns into a jog. The jog becomes a race as we begin to get a clearer view of the finish line. We strain to reach the prize (Philippians 3:13).

The race is not a sprint, but a marathon.

"Run with endurance the race that is set before us"
Hebrews 12:2.

Paul asks,
"Do you not know that those who run in a race all run, but only one receives the prize? Run in such a way that you may win" I Corinthians 9:24.

Do not be disqualified in this race. Walk faithfully. Run faithfully.

Time is running out. Soon,

"the Lord Himself will descend from heaven with a shout, with the voice of the archangel, and with the trumpet of God; and the dead in Christ shall rise first.
Then we who are alive and remain shall be caught up together with them in the air, and thus we shall always be with the Lord" I Thessalonians 4:16, 17.

As women of God, we do not have much more time to be faithful. The finish line is in sight. The Lord is coming soon. Christ Himself wants to look you in the eye and say:

"Well done, good and faithful slave; you were faithful with a few things, I will put you in charge of many things, enter into the joy of your master." Matthew 25:21, 23

Soon we will be standing together before the throne of God. It has been my prayer through this study to prepare us for that glorious moment when we see the Lord face to face. Until then, be faithful in all things.

Don't give up; there is too much at stake. Run to win.
Walk the "ancient paths" faithfully.

"Finally then, (sisters), we request and exhort you in the Lord Jesus, that, as you received from us instruction as to how you ought to walk and please God (just as you actually do walk), that you may excel still more."
I Thessalonians 4:1

"For I am confident of this very thing, that He who began a good work in you will perfect it until the day of Christ Jesus. For it is only right for me to feel this way about you all, because I have you in my heart..."
Philippians 1:6, 7

Maranatha!

Recommended Reading,
References and Resources

Chapter 1.

    The Crisis of Caring, Jerry Bridges, P & R Publishing, 1985

    The Mark of the Christian, Francis A. Schaeffer, InterVarsity Press, L'Abri
        Fellowship, 1970

    The Five Love Languages, Gary Chapman, Northfield Publishing, 1992,
        1995

Chapter 2.

    Body Dynamics, John MacArthur, Jr., Victor Books, 1982

    Body Life, Ray C. Stedman, G/L Regal Books, 1972

Chapter 4.

    Different By Design, John MacArthur, Jr., Victor Books, 1994

    Zodhiates' Complete New Testament Word Studies on Women in the Home
        and Church, Spiros Zodhiates, AMG Publishers, 1990

Chapter 6.

    "A Call to Holiness," (video), Nancy Leigh DeMoss, Life Action Ministries,
        2003

    The Heart God Purifies, Nancy Leigh DeMoss, Moody Press, 2002

    My Heart – Christ's Home, Robert Boyd Munger, InterVarsity Christian
        Fellowship, 1986

Chapter 7.

    How Should We Then Live?, Francis A. Schaeffer, Fleming H. Revell
        Company, 1976

Unless otherwise noted, all Bible quotations used in this study are taken from the
New American Standard Bible.

New American Standard Bible. Copyright 1960, 1962, 1963, 1968, 1971, 1972,
1973, 1975, 1977 by the Lockman Foundation, A Corporation Not for
Profit, La Habra, CA.

Webster's New World College Dictionary, Third Edition, Simon & Schuster, Inc.,
1997.

How to Do the *OPTIONAL Word Studies

The *OPTIONAL* word studies from each chapter are designed to enhance your understanding of each week's lesson. In order to do these *OPTIONAL* studies you will need access to some books that will broaden your ability to study the Bible for yourself.

There are two basic approaches recommended for doing your word studies.

1.   *The first approach requires two study resource books:*

·   Strong's Exhaustive Concordance of the Bible; James Strong, S.T.D., LL.D.; MacDonald Publishing Company, McLean, Virginia, 22102.

·   Vine's Complete Expository Dictionary of Old and New Testament Words; W. E. Vine, Merrill F. Unger, William White, Jr.; Copyright 1985 by Thomas Nelson Publishers.

An exhaustive concordance is a book containing every word of the text of the Bible, and every occurrence of each word in sequential order. It is important to use a concordance that is compatible with the translation version of Scripture that you are using.

Concordance words are arranged alphabetically by topic. Underneath the highlighted word that you are studying, you will find the abbreviated Bible references, in sequential order, of every place where that word is located in Scripture. Printed to the right of each reference is the text where that word is used in the Bible. To the far right of the printed text you will see a code number.

In the back of your concordance are located two dictionaries; the Old Testament dictionary is in Hebrew, and the New Testament Dictionary is in Greek. Look up the code number in the appropriate dictionary, and you will find the exact word used in the original language, along with the definition of that word.

If you would like more in-depth study of the original meaning of that word, you may use a Vine's Expository Dictionary of Old and New Testament Words. The Expository Dictionary is organized alphabetically in English, and amplifies the abbreviated definition that you will find in the back of your concordance. The code numbers located in Vine's are the same as Strong's Concordance numbers.

2. ***The second approach requires three study resource books:***

·   The Complete Word Study New Testament; Spiros Zodhiates, Th.D.; Copyright 1991 by AMG International, Inc. Publishers, Chattanooga, TN, 37422

If you would like more in-depth study of the original meaning of that word, you may use:

·   The Complete Word Study Old Testament; Spiros Zodhiates, Th.D.; Copyright 1994 by AMG International, Inc. D/B/A AMG Publishers, Chattanooga, TN, 37422

·   The Complete Word Study Dictionary New Testament; Spiros Zodhiates, Th.D.; Copyright 1992 by AMG International, Inc. Publishers, Chattanooga, TN, 37422

The Complete Word Study New and Old Testaments contain the entire Biblical texts in the King James Version. As you read the text, you will find a code number above each word. The Word Study Testaments use a numbering system that is compatible with both Vine's Expository Dictionary and Strong's Exhaustive Concordance. These numbers are all interchangeable. Look up that number in the dictionary located in the back of your Word Study Testament. There you will find the precise meaning of the word as used in the original language.

If you want further elaboration of the meaning of a New Testament word, you can use The Complete Word Study Dictionary New Testament. At this time, a Word Study Dictionary of the Old Testament has not yet been published. This New Testament dictionary is organized numerically, rather than topically, in English. Look up your code number in the dictionary to find a more in-depth definition of the word that you are studying.

Glossary

- Called – designated, invited, set apart by an action of God to some spiritual sphere and manner of being

- Confession – to agree with God by openly admitting personal guilt regarding that of which one is accused

- Faith – believing obedience; taking a promise at face value, trusting in the pledge of a person that results in responsive action

- Flesh – the unregenerate state of men; the weaker element in human nature

- Glorification – to be magnified, extolled and praised

- Glory – to ascribe honor to; to praise

- Godliness – having a heart for God that manifests itself by living in such a way that is well-pleasing to the Lord

- Gospel – the good news

- Grace – God's unmerited favor and gifts to humanity

- Holiness – set apart and dedicated to God; pure, devoted

- Justification – to be declared or pronounced righteous; acquittal

- Law – God's commandments to Israel; Mosaic Law

- Peace – wholeness and well-being in all relationships

- Propitiation – the merciful means whereby God covers and passes over man's sin, atonement

- Redemption – to purchase with a view toward one's freedom; to release on receipt of ransom

- Repentance – a change of mind about something that one has been doing wrongly, coupled with a resolve to begin doing the right thing

- Righteousness – the state of being in the right, or declared to be "not guilty"

- Saints – all those who have been set apart, holy, dedicated to God

- Salvation – spiritual and eternal deliverance given immediately by God to those who accept His conditions of repentance and faith in Jesus Christ His Son

- Sanctification – separated to God; resulting in a believer's separation from evil things and evil ways, and his being empowered to realize the will of God in his life

- Sin – "missing the mark," disobedience to Divine law

- Soul – the breath of life; the immaterial, invisible part of man; the natural life of the body including perception, feelings, intellect, personality and desires

- Sovereign – above and superior to all; supreme in power, rank, and authority; holding the position of ruler; royalty

- Spirit – the life principle bestowed on man by God; an element similar to, but higher than the soul, affecting both the soul and the body

- Wrath – God's righteous response to evil, His refusal to condone unrighteousness and His judgment upon it

About the Author

Judy Gerry met the Lord Jesus Christ as her Savior when she was a young child. During her college years at the University of California at Riverside, Judy received training through the ministry of Campus Crusade for Christ. She attended their Institute of Biblical Studies where she received in-depth Bible training from some of the nation's top seminary professors. Those classes piqued her hunger for the Word of God.

In 1969 she graduated and joined the staff of Campus Crusade for Christ. She married Dave Gerry in 1971. By 1979, their lives were bustling as the parents of five youngsters. Realizing that children are a blessing from God, Dave and Judy relished the opportunity to love and train their children. Judy's greatest desire has always been to please the Lord by being a godly wife and mother. Today, all of their grown children are believers, and Judy and Dave agree that, "I have no greater joy than to hear that my children are walking in the truth" (III John 4).

Judy and Dave were active on the board of directors for Child Evangelism Fellowship in Denver, Colorado, in the 1980s, and they were enthusiastic AWANA directors for many years. Judy continues to be active in her local Moms-in-Touch prayer group.

She has been teaching and writing Bible studies for over thirty years. Her great delight is seeing believers experience the blessings of intimacy with the Lord, and victory in their lives, as they obediently follow God's "ancient paths" (Jeremiah 6:16).

Judy and Dave are enjoying their empty-nest years in Camarillo, California, as they mentor young families in their church, teach Bible studies, speak at retreats, delight in their grandchildren, and daily anticipate the return of the Lord Jesus Christ.

Acknowledgments

This book has been a team effort before a word of it was ever written. It was written in my heart by all who have mentored me in life through taking time to lovingly teach me; even when I didn't recognize my own ignorance.

I thank and praise the Lord for all of the "Barnabas" encouragers whom He has brought into my life.

Thank You, Lord, for parents and grandparents who provided both Dave and me with foundational instruction in godly living when we were youngsters.

Thank You, Lord, for our own children whose lives continue to exhort me in pursuing godliness.

Thank You, Lord, for my husband Dave's enthusiastic support, insightful ideas, and selfless patience when I was "in the zone" while writing.

Thank You, Lord, for the staff at the Camarillo Evangelical Free Church who gave me the freedom and encouragement to write and teach this Bible study.

Thank You, Lord, for the hundreds of women whose lives have been transformed through walking the Ancient Paths. Their lives have urged me on, and they have lovingly helped me with their suggestions and passion for biblical accuracy. These women have helped to prepare this study for publication.

Thank You, Lord, for servants like Pat Papenhausen whose tireless efforts to edit this series have yielded much fruit. For Elaine Lucas and Linda Campbell, who have been true cheerleaders in initiating and facilitating the teaching of *Ancient Paths for Modern Women*. For Leigh Anne Tsuji's expertise and commitment to enhancing the fruitfulness of this ministry. For Laurie Donahue, whose vision and impetus is making these materials widely available to women.

Thank You, Lord, for Your gifted servants, Dr. Howard Hendricks and for Nancy Leigh DeMoss, who selflessly encouraged me more than they will ever know.

Lord, thank You. May these study materials help the women of our generation find "rest for their souls" as they return to the Ancient Paths. This study is from You ... use it for Your purposes and pleasure.

"For from Him and through Him and to Him are all things.
To Him be the glory forever. Amen."
Romans 11:36

Ancient Paths Ministries

Ancient Paths Ministries is committed to redirecting contemporary culture back to the timeless truths of God's Word.

With an emphasis on the practical application of Scripture to everyday living, Dave and Judy Gerry provide Bible studies and resources for spiritual growth and maturity. As authors, Bible teachers, and conference speakers, they exhort others to pursue Jesus Christ and to know Him. It is through nurturing that relationship that one will discover the foundation of all issues of life.

In addition to speaking at men's and women's conferences, Dave and Judy also lead challenging weekend marriage retreats on "How to Have an Intentional Marriage."

For more information contact:

Dave and Judy Gerry
P.O. Box 498
Somis, CA 93066-0498
(805) 484-2808

E-mail: Judy@AncientPathsMinistries.com
www.AncientPathsMinistries.com

ANCIENT PATHS
MINISTRIES
Jeremiah 6:16